Ernest W. Stint

BOTH YOUR HOUSES

BY MAXWELL ANDERSON

·PLAYS:

WHITE DESERT
(Not published)

SEA-WIFE
(Not published)

WHAT PRICE GLORY?

FIRST FLIGHT

THE BUCCANEER
(The above three plays, written in collaboration with
Laurence Stallings, published in one volume)

OUTSIDE LOOKING IN

GODS OF THE LIGHTNING
(The above two plays published in one volume.
The first is based on Jim Tully's *Beggars of Life;*
the second was written in collaboration with
Harold Hickerson)

SATURDAY'S CHILDREN

GYPSY
(Not published)

ELIZABETH THE QUEEN

NIGHT OVER TAOS

BOTH YOUR HOUSES

VERSE:

YOU WHO HAVE DREAMS

MAXWELL ANDERSON

BOTH YOUR HOUSES

A PLAY IN THREE ACTS

SAMUEL FRENCH

NEW YORK   LOS ANGELES

SAMUEL FRENCH Ltd.   LONDON

1933

First Printing March, 1933
Second Printing April, 1933
Third Printing May, 1933

MANUFACTURED IN THE UNITED STATES OF AMERICA
BY THE VAIL-BALLOU PRESS, INC., BINGHAMTON, N. Y.

Both Your Houses was first produced by the Theatre Guild at the Royale Theatre, New York, March 6, 1933. Following is a copy of the program of the first performance:

FOURTH PLAY OF THE FIFTEENTH SUBSCRIPTION SEASON

THE THEATRE GUILD, Inc.

PRESENTS

"BOTH YOUR HOUSES"

A Play in Three Acts

By MAXWELL ANDERSON

THE PRODUCTION DIRECTED BY WORTHINGTON MINER
SETTINGS DESIGNED BY ARTHUR P. SEGAL

CAST

MARJORIE GRAY .... Played by	*Aleta Freel*	
BUS .... " "	*Mary Philips*	
EDDIE WISTER .... " "	*Robert Shayne*	
SOLOMON FITZMAURICE .. " "	*Walter C. Kelly*	
MARK .... " "	*Oscar Polk*	
SIMEON GRAY .... " "	*Robert Strange*	
LEVERING .... " "	*Morris Carnovsky*	
MERTON .... " "	*John Butler*	
DELL .... " "	*William Foran*	
SNEDEN .... " "	*Jerome Cowan*	
MISS McMURTRY ...... " "	*Jane Seymour*	
WINGBLATT .... " "	*J. Edward Bromberg*	
PEEBLES .... " "	*Russell Collins*	
FARNUM .... " "	*John F. Morrissey*	
ALAN McCLEAN .... " "	*Shepperd Strudwick*	
EBNER .... " "	*Joseph Sweeney*	

ACTION AND SCENE

The play takes place in the House Office Building, Washington, D. C.

Act I

Scene 1—The office of the Chairman of the Appropriations Committee. A morning in early spring.

Scene 2—The Committee Room. The action of this scene begins three minutes before the close of Scene I.

Act II

Scene 1—The office of the Chairman of the Appropriations Committee. Late afternoon. Three days later.

Scene 2—The Committee Room. One hour later.

Act III

Scene 1—The Committee Room. Evening. Three days later.

Scene 2—The same. Three hours later.

ACT ONE

ACT ONE

Scene I

Scene: The Reception Room in the offices of the Chairman of the Appropriations Committee in the House Office Building, Washington, D.C. The entrance from the hall is at the rear. A window and the door of the Chairman's private office on the right. To the left is the door to the Appropriations Committee room. A stenographer's desk with a typewriter, telephone and a small letter file is placed on the right, and the filing case and a safe on the left.

MARJORIE GRAY, secretary to and daughter of the Chairman, is at the telephone. GRETA NILLSON, better known as BUS, enters with coat and hat on.

MARJORIE

Hello—Mr. Gray's office! Oh, hello, Alan. Where are you? The Dahl Agency? What are you doing there? But I thought you were going to be here for the meeting this morning.—You what?—You want to see Dad? Well, you can't unless you get here before they go into session and they're due right now.—Then you'd better hurry right over or you'll miss him!

BUS

Morning, Marjorie.

MARJORIE

Well, Bussy—aren't you working today?

BUS

No, dearest—I'm fired.

MARJORIE

What? What do you mean?

BUS

It was a surprise to me, too. I sat right down hard on my fifty yard line.

MARJORIE

Eddie fired you? By telephone?

BUS

By proxy. Oh, he's back from New York, but I haven't seen him.

MARJORIE

Can I do anything, do you suppose?

BUS

At the moment I don't think your dad's whole committee could. And I liked that job—and I needed it.

MARJORIE

But what's supposed to be the explanation?

BUS

It's dirty! You remember last session when Eddie was practically keeping house with the steel lobby—

MARJORIE

I remember Dad raising the devil about it—

BUS

Remember the secretary old man Sprague brought

down with him—the one that franked out that speech of Eddie's on naval parity and the Japanese menace? She came in here one day—tall, blond, never been in Washington before—

MARJORIE

Oh, yes—

BUS

Well, I think that's baby.

MARJORIE

You don't mean the steel company's moving right into the House Office Building?

BUS

Certainly— To help Mr. Wister with his home work. What else was he doing in New York? Why didn't he get back here yesterday?

MARJORIE

That's what dad wants to know.

BUS

Of course, illicit passion may have raised its pretty tousled head.

MARJORIE

Better to be swallowed by passion than by the Appalachian Steel Company. In any case you won't have trouble getting a job, Bus.

BUS

Trouble enough if I wind up with one of these new Congressmen, spending all my time cleaning up after him, and never knowing when he'll make a mess on the floor of the House.

MARJORIE

Of course the new ones don't pay quite so much—

BUS

The worst of them is they've mostly never been away from home before, and all they know about having a secretary is what they've learned from the moving pictures. They try holding you on their laps the first day and assault the second.

MARJORIE

You're romancing, Bus.

BUS

Well—you've always worked for your father, so you wouldn't know.

MARJORIE

No, I suppose not.

BUS

Not that I hold it too much against them. I'm not exactly at an age to choose my pleasures—and assault at first sight isn't always to be despised—

MARJORIE

Bus, you're a devil—

BUS

Do you know how many specimens I've had under my personal microscope? Nine. Two fired me for honesty, I fired five for dishonesty—and the other two met natural deaths by electorate. Oh wouldn't I like to get even with one or two of those corporation statesmen! Just give me half a chance, and I'm just good and sure I would.—By the way, how's your Nevada school teacher working out?

MARJORIE

Alan? He's a little out of hand! I'm going to have to give him lessons in how to juggle dynamite.

BUS

Is that all? I thought I detected adoration in his eyes!

MARJORIE

I wouldn't really mind! Adoration is rare these days —and a bit embarrassing. However—

BUS

However!

MARJORIE

I'll manage.

BUS

Of course you will.
[EDDIE WISTER *enters, a well-dressed man of thirty-eight, with a Racquet Club manner.*

EDDIE

Hello! Sorry you got here first, Bussy. Good morning, Marjorie. (MARJORIE *waves her hand.*) What did Miss Corey tell you?

BUS

Well, I got the impression, I don't know why—that I'd lost my job.

EDDIE

Why? There's plenty of work for both of you—

BUS

In Washington, maybe—

EDDIE

Don't be sour, Bus. Do you really want to know why I've taken her on?

MARJORIE

There seem to be two schools of thought.

EDDIE

Well, it's for the same reason I wasn't here yesterday. Wasn't that pretty obvious?

MARJORIE

Not at all. The committee sat here from two to five, waiting for you, and blasting your hide.

EDDIE (*to* BUS)

No kidding! Didn't you tell them I was detained?

BUS

I did. It was my last official act.

MARJORIE

Bussy didn't know you were looking for a new secretary!

EDDIE

Well, I wasn't—but I couldn't help myself. She's been the secretary of an old friend of mine.

BUS

Sure— Col. Sprague—of Appalachian Steel.

EDDIE

How did you know that?

BUS

She was down here with him last spring.

EDDIE

Look here, Bus—I'm going to need you, you know. Miss Corey doesn't know the district—nor the routine either—you'll certainly have to finish the work on the bill—

BUS

She's to be in charge of the office, isn't she?

EDDIE

I suppose so, unfortunately—

BUS

Then I'm sorry, but you'll have to excuse me. I'll take the notes in the committee, and then I'm through.

[SOLOMON FITZMAURICE *enters.*

SOL

More wenches!

MARJORIE

Good morning, Sol!

SOL

Hell-on-fire! You can't turn a corner without skirts blowing in your eye! By God, when I come up to this town it was a man's town, and a statesman could arrive at his office when he felt damn good and like

it, without a squad of females waiting for him with
their legs crossed and pads open on their knees,
yawning for dictation!

MARJORIE

Had a bad night, Sol?

SOL

In the old days, when government was government, a
couple of men could sit down over a jug of whiskey
and decide something—
[*He has opened the lower drawer of the filing case,
extracted a jug, and replaced it with another from
his satchel. The empty jug he now drops in the waste
basket.*

MARJORIE

Sol—you can't put that there!

SOL

I always have.

MARJORIE

Well, from now on it's out. The janitor's complained
about it, and threatened to report it—leave it in
your own waste-basket, darling.

SOL

And now a gentleman can't have his liquor because a
janitor complains!

EDDIE

It's only the empty ones they complain about.

SOL

Why, the lousy reds, I'll show 'em—

[*He picks up the empty jug, walks with it to the window, and drops it out.*

MARJORIE

Sol, you pig! It'll break on the coping!

SOL

Let 'em sweep it up, the Soviets! You got to bear with an old man, Clover. The changes of this world are too much for him, and he's growing testy and short-tempered.

MARJORIE

Drunk and delirious, I'd say.

SOL (*pouring a drink into a paper cup*)

On my soul, I haven't touched liquor since before breakfast.

[*There is a knock at the door and* MARK *enters with a basket piled high with letters.*

BUS

Somebody's hearing from the folks back home!

MARJORIE

Now Mark—you're not bringing all that in here?

MARK (*looking at a letter*)

Congressman Gray— Yes, ma'am.

MARJORIE (*to* BUS)

That's another night's work!

MARK

Ain't no fun for me either, Miss Marjorie.

MARJORIE

Take 'em inside, Mark.

MARK

O.K. What good is all this—that's what I want to know?

SOL

What good is it? Mark, a question like that spoken at the right time might blow this government right over, right over—don't you know that?

MARK

Tell you the truth—I don't even care. If it went over —maybe I'd be on the up-side.
[*He goes into the inner office.*

EDDIE

Call the janitor and sweep 'em out.

MARJORIE

We're not from a corporation district—we have to be pleasant to the constituents. Will you help me, Bus?

BUS

Well, come on— (*She moves toward inner office.*) My God, and they say the art of letter-writing is dead—
[*She goes in.*

MARJORIE

It is.
[*She follows* BUS *out.*

SOL

Have a little one? You're going to need it.

EDDIE

Is something hanging over me, Solomon?

SOL

When Simeon gets through with you you're going to be so low you can look up and see the depression all around you.

EDDIE

What's troubling the honorable Chairman?

SOL

Boy—
[*The door opens and* GRAY *and* LEVERING *enter from the hall.*

GRAY

Oh, there you are!

EDDIE

Morning, Simeon. Now wait—I know I'm in bad, but—

GRAY

You're a help, aren't you? One day in the term I need you here—and you choose that day to climb the Statue of Liberty.

EDDIE

No truth in it, Simeon. Merely had to go to New York. It was a crisis.

GRAY

In steel?

LEVERING

I noticed it dropped seven points!

EDDIE

Well, that may have had something to do with it.

GRAY

Well, we're a week late with this bill already, and I came back yesterday for nothing else but to get it set.

EDDIE

We'll get it set today, won't we?

GRAY

Did you even hear of a bill being put in shape in one day with a new member sitting there and asking questions?

SOL

Is that young cub coming in with the caucus today? [MARJORIE *enters from the inner office.*

LEVERING

That's just what I want to talk to you about, boys. He's been dodging me for a week now.

SOL

Dodges the party whip, does he? Well, that shows intelligence.

GRAY

Well, why—

LEVERING

That's what I'd like to know.

SOL

We're going to need a solid caucus to push this thing through the committee. You'd better get hold of him, Disraeli.

LEVERING

I've been trying to, but I can't find him.

GRAY

Don't tell me we've got another problem on our hands. The less they know the more hell they raise.

MARJORIE

Mr. McClean was just on the phone. He's on his way over here now.

GRAY

Good. You'd better see him, Dizzy, and straighten him out.

LEVERING

Isn't McClean your man, Sime? Wasn't it you brought his name up when we had that deadlock in the committee?

GRAY

I never saw him in my life, but as the case was presented to me, it looked like a set-up. He was from the district of the dam, he'd have to vote for it, and he wouldn't dare add any more to it.

SOL

What did you say his name was? McClean?

GRAY

Yes, Alan McClean.

EDDIE

The sooner we get him in and talk to him the better.

SOL

McClean. There's a McClean owns a newspaper in Nevada—used to sow a lot of headaches around here. Any relation?

GRAY

I don't know.

MARJORIE

Yes. This is his son.

SOL

If he's anything like the old man, you'd better keep him under your cold speculative eye, Dizzy.

EDDIE

Oh, we're watching him! Didn't I tell you Merton is his secretary? Well, I have an understanding with Merton.

GRAY

Well, get Merton in here and let's hear what he has to say.

[MARK *enters from the private office, crosses to the hall door and goes out.*

EDDIE

O.K. Get me Merton. Personally I think he's harmless. He doesn't know what it's all about.

SOL

Maybe.

[MARJORIE *goes into the inner office.*

EDDIE

Merton?—Wister. Come into Mr. Gray's office, will you?

SOL

About that little item of mine, Simeon. Are we going to be able to get that in?

GRAY

No, we aren't.

SOL

Give out something, Simeon! They've got to finish that dam, no matter what its name is. Everybody in Washington has tacked something onto the bill except yours truly—and I'm the one man that deserves it.

GRAY

Well, next time try to tack on something smaller than the Atlantic Fleet, and perhaps you'll get it.

EDDIE

What does he want this time?

GRAY

He wants the Atlantic Fleet to spend its vacation at that real estate development of his. How's it going to read in the newspapers—"The Atlantic Fleet is anchored for the summer at Rocky Point, Long Island, to boom Representative Fitzmaurice's summer resort and chain of speakeasies!"

SOL

The Atlantic Fleet's got to spend its summer some-

where, hasn't it? It might just as well be at Rocky
Point as at Hampton Roads, and they'd have a damn
sight better time, too. Even the navy likes good liquor,
and the girls are a hell of a lot fresher on Long
Island than down there at the naval base where the
gobs have been chasing them since 1812. We owe
something to our navy, Simeon; let 'em ashore once
in a while in a neighborhood where they won't need
prophylactics.

GRAY

Well, it carries two hundred thousand extra, and it
sounds fishy, and we can't do it.

SOL

Fishy! My God, a little honest smell of fish on that
bill would hang over it like an odor of sanctity! It's
loaded down with post offices and subsidies and river
and harbor dredging and insane asylums and smaller
miscellaneous graft till it stinks clear out on the
Pacific! That Ohio gang of Harding's was a per-
fume compared to this!

GRAY

You won't get it by arguing.

SOL

I don't know anything else you've balked at. The
bill started out as a forty million dollar appropriation to finish that goddamn dam which was supposed to cost four hundred million over all—

GRAY

You're telling me!

SOL

And which has already come to seven hundred and ninety on account of the inside gouging you stood for! Why, damn it, Simeon, you've let 'em pile odds and ends of boodle onto this last forty million until you've run it up to two hundred and seventy-five— and still going strong! There isn't a lobby in Washington that hasn't got a section all to itself! Dell's in it, Eddie's in it—

EDDIE

I am like hell—

SOL

Well, you will be if I know you! Everybody has a cut in it except old Sol himself, who did all the work. I'm the contact man for the whole kit and caboodle in this dirty House— I spend my days soft-soaping the middle-westerners and my nights drinking with the Southern colonels and my mornings eating apple pie with leather-bellies from New England—and what do I get? A rain-check—come back tomorrow!

GRAY

Too bad about you, Sol!

SOL

I'm getting to be an old man, Sime—we've worked together a long time, and I don't ask much. All I need's a jug of liquor every day and a lot of hard work. But I've got to make a little to retire on. Why, goddamn it, I haven't even paid last year's income tax yet.

GRAY

Save the goddamns for the radio. Listen, Sol, a lot of
that junk's coming out, and coming out today.
You've got to help me. They've got it loaded down
till the old man'll have to veto his own measure. Anyway, we're not going to be caught short in front of
any new member—

[MERTON, *a sharp-faced young man, enters without
preliminaries.*

MERTON

Morning—

GRAY

—and you can lay that to Eddie and his New York
crisis.

EDDIE

Hello, Merton. Come in and tell us what you know
about McClean. Mr. Levering is worried about him.

MERTON

Oh, I wouldn't be, sir. He's a nice fellow.

LEVERING

No doubt, but what's his history?

MERTON

Tell you that in a nut-shell. He was a teacher in an
agricultural college in Nevada. Kicked up a row over
the misappropriation of endowment funds—hell of a
stink—got himself fired. His father made an issue
of it in his paper—and the upshot was, elected to
Congress. Tell me he ran a pretty smart campaign,

too. But he wouldn't have been elected if a lot of contractors hadn't got back of him and put up the funds.

GRAY

Oh, he's in with the contractors?

MERTON

No, he isn't. He's straight. It never enters that head not to be straight. But the farmers out there are waiting for water, and he promised them he'd work to get the Nevada dam finished. He'll be for the bill. You needn't worry about that.

EDDIE

Good.

GRAY

What's he like?

MERTON

Serious. Wears mail-order clothes. Reads Thomas Jefferson. He came down to Washington three months ago, and he's spent all his time in the Congressional Library.

LEVERING

But that doesn't answer my question, Mr. Merton. What's he doing that is so important that he can't make an appointment with me?

MERTON

That's the funny thing about it. You won't believe this. He's been working day and night having his own election investigated.

[*A pause.*

SOL

Say that again.

MERTON

That's true. He's having his own election investigated.

SOL

Now for the love of— How?

MERTON

He's having a detective agency look it up.

SOL

At his own expense?

MERTON

At his own expense.

SOL

Comes from Nevada, intellectual, reads Jefferson, having his own election investigated. Simeon, call your meeting to order and for God's sake muzzle him. This is William Jennings Bryan!
[*He goes into the committee room.*

MERTON

Leave him to me, Mr. Gray. I'll steer him right.

EDDIE

Are you staying right with him, Merton?

MERTON

I follow him—and he believes everything I tell him. Just leave him to me.

LEVERING

Is he in his office now?

MERTON

Not yet sir.

LEVERING

Well, when he comes in, will you tell him again and very definitely that I want to see him at once in my office?

MERTON

Yes, sir.
[*They go out.*

GRAY

Marjorie, will you come with me. (MARJORIE *and* GRAY *start toward the inner office.* DELL, SNEDEN *and* MISS MCMURTRY *enter from the hall.*) Go right in, everybody—be with you in a minute.
[*He and* MARJORIE *go into the office.*

DELL

So you got here at last!

SNEDEN

We were meeting in Washington, you know—not in New York.

EDDIE

I'm damned sorry, boys—

DELL

Well, you're only a day late—

MCMURTRY

We waited all afternoon, Mr. Wister. I must say—

EDDIE

I'm awfully sorry, Miss McMurtry, you must be-lieve me—

MCMURTRY

I suppose I'll have to—

DELL

After all, what's twenty-four hours?
[GRAY *reenters from the office.*

SNEDEN

I could have shot eighteen holes yesterday—

EDDIE

You couldn't walk eighteen holes—
[*They all go into the committee room.* WINGBLATT,
PEEBLES *and* FARNUM *enter from the hall.*

WINGBLATT

Well, why shouldn't Nevada get it?

FARNUM

Now, wait a minute! You Easterners treat California
like a foreign country! If they let those Fresno banks
fail, the whole Imperial Valley'll fail—California'll
go straight to hell and the moving pictures along
with it—

WINGBLATT

That's a good idea too.
[BUS *enters from the inner office.*

PEEBLES

The whole South went to hell after the Civil War,

and nobody seemed to care much— We've been unemployed since 1865 and we get along, don't we?

BUS

Go right in, gentlemen, the meeting's beginning.

WINGBLATT

You're a complaining man, Peebles. I don't know
what to do about you!
[*The men pass into the committee room.* ALAN MC-
CLEAN *enters from the hall.*

BUS

Good morning, Mr. McClean.

ALAN

Good morning, Miss Nillson.

BUS

Looking for someone? She's in there.

ALAN

Thanks. I hope things haven't started yet.

BUS

Oh, the hyenas are in conference. I've already missed
words of wisdom.
[BUS *goes into the committee room.* MARJORIE *comes
out of the inner office.*

MARJORIE

Hello, Alan. Do you know people are looking for
you?

ALAN

Who?

MARJORIE

Levering, for one.

ALAN

Oh, he's been looking for me for days. Am I too late to see your father?

MARJORIE

I'm afraid so. The committee's in session. You should have been here an hour ago.

ALAN

I did my best. I got some information yesterday which had to be verified, and it took time—it took all night.

MARJORIE

And that's why I haven't seen you—

ALAN

Yes. It's something I'm not quite ready to talk about yet.

MARJORIE

Not even with me?

ALAN

Not even with you.

MARJORIE

Well, you are late, but it can't be helped now. You'll have to walk in and sit down and tell them who you are.

ALAN

I think I'd better meet your father first and get

started regularly. I'm not at all sure I know how to deal with these facts I've gathered. That's why I tried to see him yesterday.

MARJORIE

He simply couldn't manage it, Alan. He'd just got back and didn't have a free moment. Most of this bill was framed while he was ill and away, and it was a day's work checking up on it.

ALAN

Then—there might be some clauses he hasn't had time to look into?

MARJORIE

Oh, that's possible—there are an awful lot of clauses.

ALAN

I see. I'd better see him before I sit on the committee.

MARJORIE

You mean—you mean you aren't going in today?

ALAN

No, I don't think so.

MARJORIE

Merton's been advising you, hasn't he? They know about you, Alan. And if some of them didn't have a lot of faith in you why would you be here at all?

ALAN

I wouldn't be too sure that's the reason. They may have wanted somebody that looked easy and didn't know too much.

MARJORIE

Do you think you're like that?

ALAN

I probably don't know how to be very dangerous,
even if I do know more than they think I do. And
appointments are made that way sometimes, aren't
they?

MARJORIE

All the time. I played among the pork barrels as a
child! That's what one learns. In fact, you're quite
right. Yours was made that way.

ALAN

Well, I don't like it—really Marjorie.

MARJORIE

Dad will take you right under his wing, Alan, and
help you any way he can. He's like that.

ALAN

I know—I know. I've been counting on him.
[LEVERING enters from the hall.

LEVERING

Ah, there you are, McClean. I've been looking for
you!

ALAN

How are you, Mr. Levering?

LEVERING

Just a little perturbed, if you don't mind my saying
so. I wanted to have a chat with you before you took
up your duties on the committee.

ALAN

Oh, I'm sorry.

LEVERING (*to* MARJORIE)

My dear—could Mr. McClean and I have a word in private anywhere?

MARJORIE (*looking at her notes*)

Oh, I have some calls to make— I don't think you'll be interrupted here.
[*She goes into the inner office.*

LEVERING

Thank you, my dear—we won't be a minute. Well, young man, no doubt you've been amusing yourself?

ALAN

I've been studying a little—

LEVERING

Hard at your books as usual? Didn't you miss an appointment with the committee yesterday?

ALAN

Yes, I did.

LEVERING

Now I don't know what your ideas are, my boy, but a good party man doesn't make important decisions, as a rule, without consulting his party leaders—

ALAN

I'm not really sure I am a good party man, Mr. Levering.

LEVERING

What? You were elected on a reform ticket, I know.

But you don't want to count as one of these sons of
the wild jackass, do you?

ALAN

I don't especially like the name—no.

LEVERING

If you want to get anything done you have to cooperate.

ALAN

I know that.

LEVERING

But you don't cooperate, McClean. We knew you
were a sensible, reliable young man, and we put you
on the Appropriations Committee for that reason. I
had one talk with you and then you disappeared. I
haven't seen you. You've either avoided me, or I've
had unbelievable luck with the telephone service.
Now what's the matter?

ALAN

I guess I've just been uncertain of a number of things
—and I didn't want to try to talk about them till I
felt sure—

LEVERING

That's a good answer. I can see your point of view.
But if you're puzzled, just put your questions to
me. Now the caucus this morning is considering the
deficiency bill for the Nevada dam. You're naturally
for that project; it'll make a nice start for you.

ALAN

Well, I don't know—

LEVERING

You don't know what?

ALAN

I've discovered that some of the people who backed me for office were the contractors who have handled the work on the whole project.

LEVERING

Can you be sure of that?

ALAN

Oh yes. I've looked it up and they don't really need forty millions to finish it. There's a lot of water in this business besides what's to be used for irrigation.

LEVERING

If you're sure of that, we ought to go over it. We certainly should. And I want to do it.

ALAN

But I didn't want to go over it with anyone, Mr. Levering. And I felt almost certain that if I went over it with you, it would lead to a compromise.

LEVERING

You amaze me, McClean. There could be no question of compromise in such a case. This comes of your working alone and taking no advice.

ALAN

It puts me in a sort of hyphenated position, because I realize I owe it to the people who elected me to put the dam through. But I also ran on an economy plat-form, and that concerns the whole country. I've been thinking about it a good deal and the two things just don't go together. But I guess I'll just have to decide that for myself.

LEVERING

The dam must go through, of course.
[*The telephone bell rings.*

ALAN

But why must there be so many expensive and unnecessary things attached to it?

LEVERING

You wouldn't break your word to the people? That would be flatly dishonest.

ALAN

But isn't the whole affair dishonest? (MARJORIE *enters and goes to the phone.*)

MARJORIE

Hello— Yes.

LEVERING

Now, look here—

MARJORIE

I'm sorry—he's in conference.

LEVERING

We must go over your information in detail. Suppose you come with me now?

ALAN

I'm sorry but there's another matter I must take care of first.

LEVERING

How long will it take?

ALAN

About half an hour, I think.

LEVERING

Very well, I'll expect you in my office in half an hour. [*He goes out.*

MARJORIE

Anything unpleasant?

ALAN

He seemed to find it so.

MARJORIE

What led up to it?

ALAN

I told him I hadn't consulted him on a certain matter because I didn't want his advice.

MARJORIE

You said that? To Levering? Why, you couldn't have been more insulting!

ALAN

Well, it just happened—I suppose if I'd been better prepared, but I couldn't think of how to get around it—

MARJORIE

You've got to keep on good terms with him. He's the presidential mouthpiece—the official whipper-in of the administration.

ALAN

I could bring myself to dislike him. I don't like taking

advice from him and I don't like his face. And I certainly don't care to be—whipped in.

MARJORIE

But Alan—

ALAN

I've changed my mind. I think I'll sit with the committee after all.

MARJORIE

But you have an appointment with Levering—

ALAN

I didn't make an appointment. If he did, he can keep it. What's it like in there? A table—with chairs around it?

MARJORIE

That's right.

ALAN

There'll be an extra chair, I hope.

MARJORIE

Oh, yes.

ALAN

We're having lunch together, aren't we?

MARJORIE

Yes.

ALAN

Here goes.

MARJORIE

Alan, you aren't a wild radical, are you?

ALAN

No, just a farmer.

MARJORIE

Well, this first time it might be better just to listen.

ALAN

Oh, I'm not going to say anything.

MARJORIE

All right!

CURTAIN

ACT ONE

Scene II

Scene: The Committee Room. A large entrance at the rear, the office door at the right.

The Committee, with GRAY *presiding, is seated around the table.* GRAY *is speaking.* BUS *sits at his left taking notes.*

GRAY

Also, in my humble opinion, subject to correction from superior minds, Section 42 had better be struck out in toto, just to avoid possible remarks from the gallery. When you want money for river dredging it's better to pick a stream that doesn't dry up completely in the summer. I don't insist that your rivers be navigable, but it would look better if they had water in them.

PEEBLES

Isn't that the Big Belly Creek improvement?

GRAY

That's it.

PEEBLES

Well, listen, Mr. Chairman, we had to concede that to get the majority for the Iowa drainage business. It's going to mess up a lot of deals if that's out.

36

GRAY

And now who wants Iowa drained?

PEEBLES

That's the jackass Senator's pet notion, Simeon. It seems there's some of Iowa under water, and he wants to put up levees and drain it. I've never been in Iowa myself.

GRAY

The jackass, huh. I don't suppose there happens to be any patronage mixed up in that?

PEEBLES

Well, there you are.

GRAY

All right. I suppose we'll have to leave that in. Section 74, enlarging the nursing force under the Department of the Interior. I suppose you'll have the appointing of those nurses, Miss McMurtry?

MCMURTRY

Why, as a matter of fact, they do usually ask me for the names—

GRAY

I'm sorry—but that's out.

MCMURTRY

Why, Mr. Gray!

GRAY

It's out, Miss McMurtry.

MCMURTRY

But those nurses are so badly needed! You have no

idea of the problems of the maternity bureau. In the first place—

GRAY

Let's not go into them now.

MCMURTRY

I suppose it's because I'm a woman, and—

GRAY

It's more than that; this section has been changed since I saw it last. What does this mean, this addendum, allotting fifteen thousand for the dissemination of birth control information and contraceptives?

SOL

Why look at me?

GRAY

Don't you know that's clearly against the law?

MCMURTRY

Only in cases of real necessity, Mr. Chairman. You see, so much of the difficulty in maternity cases arises from too many children, and after devoting years to a study of the subject I have formed the deliberate opinion that one should strike at the seat of the trouble.

SNEDEN

That certainly is the seat of it!

MCMURTRY

Moreover, I don't consider it a subject for jesting— especially at a time when so many men are unemployed and are constantly at home and women don't know how to protect themselves and the result is even more mouths to feed and even greater destitution!

PEEBLES

I declare that angle never occurred to me before—

MCMURTRY

There are a lot of things that don't occur to men, but women know that during periods of unemployment the men have nothing else to do and no other outlet for their energy.

WINGBLATT

What!

PEEBLES

Energy!

MCMURTRY

It's purely scientific—

GRAY

Genius, Miss McMurtry. Downright genius. Nevertheless, that section is out in entirety. Mr. Farnum, what was the reason you gave for wanting to establish a national park around the home of Joaquin Miller? Who was Joaquin Miller?

FARNUM

Didn't he write poetry?

GRAY

I'm asking you. I don't know whether he wrote poetry or a joke-book.

WINGBLATT

Certainly he wrote poetry. "Sail on! Sail on! Sail on!"

GRAY

Is that all you remember, Mr. Wingblatt?

WINGBLATT

That's all.

GRAY

Then that's out.

FARNUM

Suit yourself. You lose three opposition votes on the St. Lawrence if you drop it, though.

GRAY

We can afford it. And 65 is out.

EDDIE

What's 65?

GRAY

Establishing a patrol of the Canadian border for the Japanese beetle.

WINGBLATT

What! Oh, say, listen—

GRAY

Who wants it?

WINGBLATT

Some of the Non-Partisan League and Farmer-Labor contingent. They want to employ a lot of farmers.

GRAY

Do we need the Non-Partisans to push this bill through, Dell?

DELL

Not according to my figures.

GRAY

Then we'll drop that.

SOL

Now wait! What makes you think Dell's figures are better than mine? I say we do need 'em—and what's more those pretty little golden bugs are a god-send. They're coming down like a plague from the north-west, and it gives us a chance to control the Non-Partisans by voting a little something to exterminate 'em.

DELL

They're coming from the southwest, Sol, not the northwest. There are no Japanese beetles along the Canadian border.

SOL

Well, what of it? Is this geography or politics?

GRAY

If Dell says we don't need 'em, they're out, and that's that.

SOL

Just the watch-dog of the Treasury, earning his name.

GRAY

Sol, I promised the President to bring this one down

under two hundred millions and we're going to do it. You can outvote me on it if you want to, but if you do I swear I'll attack it on the floor and have it sent back here.

SOL

I've got no deal on with the Non-Partisans, Simeon! They're no friends of mine!

GRAY

Then why are they bombarding me with arguments against leaving the Atlantic Fleet at Hampton Roads this summer?

SOL

How would I know? Maybe they've got children on some of those vessels and they want 'em protected—

GRAY

Well, you can hardly blame me if it puts me on my guard—

SOL

By God, if there's anything I hate more than store liquor it's an honest politician! There's something slimy about a man being honest in your position. You spend your days and nights arranging deals among a pack of thieves, and just because you won't take anything for yourself, you think your hands are clean.

GRAY (*busy with his papers*)

I get the impression you're talking a lot, Sol.

SOL

The whole damn government's a gang of liver flukes,

sucking the blood out of the body politic—and there
you sit, an honest liver fluke, arranging the graft
for everybody else and refusing to do any blood
sucking on your own account! God, it makes me sick!

MCMURTRY

Mr. Fitzmaurice—there are some of us here who
would rather not be compared to animal parasites—
and moreover the government is here for the good
of the people! It does a great deal of good—

SOL

It does a four billion dollar business in taxes, and
I'll say that's pretty good. For God's sake why don't
you folks admit it, and take your bribes like men
and go home and invest 'em?

GRAY

You all through, Sol?

SOL

No!

GRAY

Section 57—I don't find it in this copy. Lend me
your notes, Dell. (*He looks at* DELL's *copy.* ALAN
enters. They all look up.) Yes?

ALAN

I'm—I'm Mr. McClean.

GRAY

My name's Gray. Do you want to meet the members
of the committee?

ALAN

I don't want to disturb anything. I'll just listen, thank you.
[*He sits.*

GRAY

Why, surely.
[*A smile goes around the Committee.*

SOL

Young man, my name's Fitzmaurice, Solomon Fitzmaurice, and I welcome you to our festive board. You'll find us all too damned friendly here.

ALAN

Thank you.

GRAY

Section 57—yes, that's the one. That's out.

DELL

But listen, Sime, that's the new veterans' hospital at Baton Rouge.

GRAY

Right.

DELL

Well—that—you'd better think twice about that, Sime.

GRAY

I understand that hospital isn't really needed—

DELL

No, but you see—

FARNUM

Oh Sime—have you got a copy of the bill? Mr. McClean would like to look up certain items.

GRAY

Certainly. Take mine.

[*He hands it over.* ALAN *studies it, turning the pages.*

DELL

I don't quite see how that can be eliminated, after our very definite talk with Klein.

GRAY

I. J.? Is that Klein's district?

DELL

It is, indeed—and you remember what the Legion told him—

GRAY

Yes, I see. Well, we'll have to make up for it somewhere else. That'll have to stay in.

DELL

Right.

GRAY

But for God's sake give me a hand with some of these cuts, some of you. There's about thirty-three million still to come out.

WINGBLATT

What are you going to eliminate? You've cut enough already to get it killed in the Senate—

GRAY

It'll pass the Senate—

PEEBLES

It may not even get by the House if you pare it any
more.

GRAY

It's got to come down, I tell you! Whether the House
likes it or not, it's got to get used to spending less
money.

WINGBLATT

It can't be done!

GRAY

It's going to be done! There's no way of raising the
money! Talk to the Ways and Means Committee!

WINGBLATT

Oh, hell.

GRAY

Section 200. Appropriating an additional million for
extending irrigation service from the Nevada dam.
That can go over to the next session.

ALAN

Mr. Chairman—

GRAY

Yes?

ALAN

Could I have a word?

GRAY

I can tell you right now, Mr. McClean, that section's
out, but go ahead.

ALAN

It wasn't my intention, Mr. Gray, to argue about the appropriation, but there are a few questions I would like to ask.

SOL

I knew it!

GRAY

It's all right. Don't mind us.

ALAN

What I wanted to ask was—

EDDIE

Louder, please.

ALAN

What I wanted to ask was—am I correct in assuming two hundred millions is the total which the bill will carry?

GRAY

I hope so.

ALAN

And is it the intention of the committee to put the bill in final shape today?

GRAY

Yes—that's what we're shooting at.

ALAN

Oh—well I just want to say, Mr. Chairman, that I'm in sympathy with you on this. When you say the bill ought to be cut down, I agree with you. But I'd go farther than that. I think the whole bill—and I hope you'll realize that I say this quite sincerely— not for effect at all—and I know it's a radical suggestion—but I think the whole bill ought to be dropped.

SOL

Now that's something!
[*There is a general gasp.*

WINGBLATT

You'll have to take that up somewhere else, sir.

ALAN

I think it ought to be dropped right here and now.

GRAY

You've made a study of this, I presume?

ALAN

I've been looking into it for some time, Mr. Chairman.

GRAY

I have been in charge of House appropriations for something like fifteen years, sir, and I say that this bill can't be dropped, and it's like sweating blood to get it down within limits. If you have any suggestions along that line—

ALAN

I come from an agricultural district, Mr. Chairman, where the farmers haven't got any money, and they're taxed beyond what they can stand already. Not only that but in the town I come from there used to be

thirty-eight stores on the main street. There are now
fifteen—because people have no money to buy. When
stores get judgments against the farmers and put
up their cattle and machinery at auction, nothing is
sold. And the whole country's like that. Nobody can
buy anything, at any price. Now, I was elected and
sent here because I told my people I'd do what I
could to reduce taxes and cut down even necessary
expenditures. And there's nothing in this bill that
can't be done without. So I'm against it.

GRAY

We'll take the vote later. If you wish to vote against
it, that's your privilege. Meanwhile, we have little
enough time, and I'd like to proceed with the business
in hand.

ALAN

I beg your pardon, Mr. Chairman, but I thought
this was the business in hand.

GRAY

At the moment you're out of order.

WINGBLATT

Do you expect to run the House and dictate to the
government the first time you step into a committee
room?

ALAN

It may be that I've had exceptional opportunities for
studying this particular bill. You see, in looking up
a certain matter that concerned me closely I was
astonished to come upon several instances of lobbyist

influence. There's private graft in this bill, Mr. Chairman.

SOL

My God, that's a bombshell!

GRAY

What do you mean, Mr. McClean?

ALAN

I mean that in at least three instances, the people who are asking for certain appropriations stand to benefit in a monetary way.

GRAY

Will you kindly name the sections concerned?

ALAN

Well—the gentlemen I mean are no doubt aware of the situation. They are on this committee.

SOL (*rising*)

By the eternal, we'll have their heart's blood! I been suspecting for years there was something crooked going on here!

GRAY

Sit down, Sol. You'll have to make your charges a little more concrete, Mr. McClean, if you expect any credence.

ALAN

Well, that's a little difficult. I prefer not to do that at present.

GRAY

Then you'll pardon us if the committee goes ahead with its program.

DELL

I happen to be somewhat familiar with your campaign for office in Nevada, Mr. McClean. It seems to me that you pledged yourself to work for the completion of the Nevada dam. Am I correct?

ALAN

Yes.

DELL

Then you must know that this bill was framed for the special purpose of supplying funds to complete that dam.

ALAN

Well, yes, but I am no longer in favor of it.

DELL

No?

ALAN

I have discovered that my backer and campaign manager had an understanding concerning the contracts. Naturally that puts a different face on the scheme.

SOL

Why don't you ask him why, some of you gouging miscreants, lost to honor and truth! I fear we stand alone here, Mr. McClean, absolutely alone!

ALAN

Pardon me, Mr. Fitzmaurice, but you are one of the gentlemen I had in mind. There is an appropriation listed here in connection with the maintenance of the Atlantic Fleet.

SOL

They took it away from me—took it away from an old man—and here I stand in my honesty—naked to every breeze! Everybody else gets his pickings, but old Sol gets shoved away from the trough. It's nothing less than conspiracy!

ALAN

Are you also making charges against the committee?

SNEDEN

Wait a minute! Let me ask you something, Mr. McClean. You say we should drop this whole bill. You must know that that Nevada dam is a half billion dollar investment, and it's been waiting there for a year and a half for this forty millions to finish it.

PEEBLES

Three thousand people stranded in construction camps!

WINGBLATT

A hundred thousand farmers waiting for water!

SNEDEN

What's more, they're your own constituents!

MCMURTRY

No wonder the stores are closed on your own main street!

DELL

And after all you owe something to your district.

ALAN

But I say there's an understanding with the contractors! That forty million is too much because the
work could be done for less if the bidding were honest!
And even if the whole forty millions were necessary,
why must the bill carry over two hundred millions
for other projects—most of them quite unnecessary—

WINGBLATT

How unnecessary?

ALAN

Wasteful, useless, extravagant, ridiculous—

WINGBLATT

And how are you going to pass a bill giving forty
millions to Nevada if the rest of the country gets
nothing out of it? Nobody'd vote for it but Nevada's
own Congressmen and by God you'd look pretty
lonely.

ALAN

Does Congress have to be bribed to pass a bill?

SOL

Boy, they're laughing at you. Maybe I'm laughing
at you myself. Don't you know about the government of the United States?

GRAY

That's enough, Sol.

SOL

Sime, this boy is suffering!

GRAY

I say it's enough.

SOL

Wait a minute. Let me put it to him in two words. Mr. McClean, you can't do anything in Congress without arranging matters. Everybody wants something, everybody's trying to put something over for his voters, or his friends, or the folks he's working for. So they all get together, and they put all those things in bills, and everybody votes for 'em. All except the opposition. They don't vote for 'em because they don't get anything. That's all there is to it. That's the whole government. Is that crooked?

ALAN

Yes, it is.

SOL

That's what I say. I've been saying it for years. (*The committee laughs.*) What are you laughing at? You all came up to this Congress fighting mad, full of juice and high purpose—just like him. Well, look what happened to you. You run into people making deals! Money changers in the temple of public righteousness!

MCMURTRY

Indeed!

SOL

Yes, and it happened to me too, and I was shocked

and I started making radical remarks. Why, before
I knew where I was I was an outsider. I couldn't
get anything for my district, I couldn't get recognized to make a speech—I couldn't even get
into a poker game. My constituents complained
and I wasn't going to be re-elected. So I began
to play ball, just to pacify the folks back
home. And it worked. They've been re-electing me
ever since—re-electing a fat crook because he gets
what they want out of the Treasury, and fixes the
Tariff for 'em, and sees that they don't get gypped
out of their share of the plunder. That's what
happened to every man of us here, but that's the
way the government's run. If you want to be in
Congress you have to do it. You let us finish that
dam for you, and you'll be re-elected—talk against
it and you won't be.

MCMURTRY

I won't listen to this!
[*Half the committee is standing.*

ALAN

What right have I to think about being re-elected?

SOL

I'm saying it only because you're going to make
yourself a lot of trouble, boy. If you don't fall in
line and help pass the pie—and do it quick—you'll
be no better than a ghost in these historic halls.
Nobody'll see you or hear what you say—and when
you leave it'll be as if you'd never been here.

ALAN

Maybe it's been so in the past—but I can't believe it's true now. Times are different—the people—

SOL

All right, look around you and see how many friends you've got among us. Talk to 'em—ask 'em how many'll support you in blocking a bill or even cutting it down! State your principles!

ALAN

Mr. Chairman!

GRAY

I'm through! Go on—talk your heads off!

ALAN

I'm sorry this came up this way, Mr. Chairman, and members of the Committee—but I didn't expect to say anything today. I came here really to sit and listen. So I've probably gone at everything wrong end to and broken all the rules there are—but now it's started I would like to ask you something. Isn't it true the country's pretty desperate about taxes now—and wouldn't it do more good than harm to cancel this bill? There may be necessary expenses in it, and I know my own district stands to benefit more than any other—but when you just haven't got any money, you have to do without what you've been used to.

SNEDEN

Well, this country has long been in need of some bright young college graduate who was willing to take over the burdens of the administration.

MCMURTRY

Young man, you've been dreadfully misled.

ALAN

I think maybe you've all been misled for a long time—you think there's still money to spend—but there isn't, and you're all going to find it out!

DELL

Meeting over, Simeon?

GRAY

Adjourned till tomorrow. Usual time.

FARNUM

Wait a minute, Hi. I want to see you.

PEEBLES

It's all gone. I tell you.
[*The members have begun to straggle out.* ALAN *watches them go until only* SOL *and* GRAY *remain.* BUS *is still at the table putting papers together.*

SOL

Want to talk it over with me, McClean?

ALAN

No. I—I'd rather be alone for a while.

SOL

Do you ever take a drink in the middle of the day?

ALAN

No thanks.

SOL

All right, all right—only don't make a virtue of it.
[*He goes out.*

GRAY

All right, Miss Nillson, Marjorie will take it over
tomorrow.
[BUS *goes out.*

ALAN

Mr. Gray.

GRAY

Yes?

ALAN

I wanted to see you before the meeting—

GRAY

I'll make it just as soon as I can, McClean, but at
this moment I'm helpless. Do me a favor. Talk to
Miss Gray about it.

ALAN

I need somebody's help very much, Mr. Gray, and
I'd rather it was you than anybody else—

GRAY

You will need help if you're to carry through your
program. More help than I can give you.

ALAN

I've been led to believe that you'd be in sympathy
with me.

GRAY

I am. But I would suggest that you've been a bit

too heavy-handed to be effective. We all get hot
about things when we're first here, McClean. But it
doesn't help any, and after a while we find out that—

ALAN

I know I should apologize for the mess I made of it,
but I really wasn't prepared to broach the matter
at all, and besides I was bothered by the fact that
some of my evidence might seem to reflect—well, on
even your integrity.

[MARJORIE *has entered from the office.*

GRAY

My integrity?

ALAN

Yes, sir.

GRAY

Well, that's something I've always taken care of
myself, my boy, and I can't remember that anything's ever been said against it. You have the advantage of novelty.

ALAN

I realize that you were away at the time the bill was
framed, but I have it on fairly competent authority
that you own stock in a Culver bank, which is in
shaky condition, and that the location of a penitentiary there and the spending of federal money would
probably save it.

GRAY

I hadn't thought of that, but now you mention it, I
hope it does save it.

ALAN

But if all this came out it might look strange—

GRAY

You think so?

ALAN

And it's such a simple thing to eliminate——

GRAY

Sometimes it's not so simple, McClean.

ALAN

But, Mr. Gray, if I really make a fight on this bill, I'll have to use all the ammunition I've got—

GRAY

If there's anything wrong with the penitentiary at Culver, Mr. McClean, I'll be glad to go over it with you, but not just now, please. It's an asylum, isn't it, an asylum for the criminal insane?

ALAN

Yes.

GRAY

Yes, I remember. But it had slipped my mind that it went to Culver. You know, I think I met your father when he was in Washington once. Not exactly a patient man himself, but valuable. You ought to have some gift for politics if you're like him.

ALAN

I hope I'm not impatient.

GRAY

You are, though. Now, shall we say as soon as possible? At the very earliest opportunity?

ALAN

Yes, sir. Thank you.
[*He goes out.*

MARJORIE

Was he right? Is the bank really in bad condition?

GRAY

I don't know of any bank in good condition.

MARJORIE

Then it could be made to look—strange?

GRAY

I suppose it could. The papers would go after it like a pack of wolves. Oh, a lot of people would have plenty of fun believing I was crooked. You look as if you half believed it yourself.

MARJORIE

No, darling. But the penitentiary had better go somewhere else.

GRAY

That's a difficulty. It's hooked up with so many agreements and promises. It's a week's work to untangle a thing like that. Maybe we shouldn't have laughed at his detectives!

MARJORIE

Maybe I shouldn't have made out such a good case

for his appointment. How did you ever let that
penitentiary clause slip by?

GRAY

That thing was fixed up while I was away, Marjorie,
and there wasn't much point in ruling it out because
it benefited my home town. That would have been
bending backwards. Well, I guess you have to bend
backwards in this business.

MARJORIE

I knew it was something like that. You shouldn't be
working so hard.

GRAY

I'll have a few minutes for lunch if you could go out
with me now.

MARJORIE

I had a—no, I'll go with you. I'll put a few things
away here while you get your coat.

GRAY

Be right with you.
[*He goes out.* ALAN *enters from the hall.*

ALAN

Are we going to lunch, Marjorie? I didn't tell you
what was on my mind, because it seemed best to talk
to him about it.

MARJORIE

I don't know what you think you're here for nor what
you want to do, but you've forfeited my respect for
whatever it is.

ALAN

Why?

MARJORIE

And it's not that he's my father, but he's the one
person who's really on your side! He's fought all his
life to cut down appropriations and maintain a
standard of honesty! And he's never got anything
out of it.

ALAN

But I always believed that, Marjorie.

MARJORIE

But the first step you take in your campaign is to
turn on him! Threatening to expose an innocent co-
incidence that would make it impossible for him to go
on with his work! Don't you know every form of
corruption in the country would take on new life if
he were crowded off the committee? Don't you know
every lobbyist in the city's waiting for just such a
chance?

ALAN

But Marjorie—if he's made himself a part of the
system so much that I can't attack any part of it
without attacking him, I can't help it.

MARJORIE

But he hasn't! He isn't part of it. The clause means
nothing to him personally, but it can't be thrown out
at the last minute?

ALAN

He told you that?

MARJORIE

Yes. It might look as if he were to blame if it were brought out. But it would be unfair, terribly unfair. You don't know how hard it is to keep up a reputation like his over a long period of years in Washington.

ALAN

But Marjorie, I do realize it.

MARJORIE

Did you actually set detectives on him?
[BUS and GRAY *enter from the office.*

ALAN

No, I didn't.

MARJORIE

Then how did you know all this?

ALAN

Oh, it doesn't matter.

GRAY

Well, Marjorie.

MARJORIE

Yes—let's go.
[GRAY *and* MARJORIE *go out together.*

BUS

I beg your pardon.

ALAN

It's all right.

BUS

I thought I heard a repercussion as I came in here.

ALAN

You did.

BUS

It sounded final. I hope it wasn't.

ALAN

I don't know.

BUS

That's no way to win a girl, you know. Opposing her father.

ALAN

No. I know it isn't.

BUS

I wish I'd met somebody like you when I was young and inflammable. I'd be a better woman today. However, now that I'm here, let me congratulate you on your disgraceful conduct in the committee. You were swell.

ALAN

Was I?

BUS

I haven't heard such a row since the debate over taking the couches out of the House Office Building. That was an uproar.

ALAN

I suppose I might as well go ahead with it.

BUS

With what?

ALAN

Well, I'm against this bill—it's crooked from beginning to end—and I've got enough information to
kill it.

BUS

Where, if I may ask, did you get all this stuff?

ALAN

Well, I was having my election investigated.

BUS

I heard that—I didn't believe it.

ALAN

Well, I was. And day before yesterday I got some
extra pages from the bureau—and they weren't
about myself—they were about some of the others
on the committee.

BUS

Someone else is doing some investigating.

ALAN

Yes. Well, they sent right over for the pages but
not before I'd read them. I didn't realize at first
how important it was, but now that I do, I'm certainly going to use it.

BUS

How?

ALAN

On the floor of the House, if necessary.

BUS

But what gave you the idea they'd let you make a speech?

ALAN

Why not?

BUS

They've got machinery down here especially designed for keeping people from speaking. No, you won't get a chance to open your mouth. The Speaker'll be tipped off, the parliamentary experts will have your number, they'll know everything you're planning to say before you say it. Why, damn it, your own secretary is working for them and turning in regular reports.

ALAN

My secretary? Merton?

BUS

Yes, Merton.

ALAN

But that can't be.

BUS

It is, I assure you.

ALAN

And you think I won't be allowed to speak?

BUS

I know you won't. Alan, you're up against a gang of professional empire wreckers. If you added up the conquerors of all time, from Alexander to Napoleon, the lump of what they got wouldn't touch what's dragged down annually by this gang out of our national treasury. And that being the case, do you think they'd hesitate to make things difficult for you? So far as they're concerned, you just aren't here. You don't exist. You aren't even a fly in the ointment. And the ointment business around here runs, believe me, into something staggering.

ALAN

I guess I might just as well go home.

BUS

You might just as well. It's a bad time for idealists. I'm out of a job myself.

ALAN

And everybody just lets them sit here—ruining things! Why, who are they, anyway? Who gives orders like that?

BUS

Oh, those on the inside—

ALAN

And anybody that isn't on the inside is supposed to stand around and wait till they give the word?

BUS

Yes, indeed.

ALAN

By God, I'm not as easy as that. And I won't do it! No, and I'm not going home—

BUS

No, you'll stay and draw your salary. They all do. They've done it for years.

ALAN

They won't drive me out, and they won't give me orders! I know how the country feels whether they do or not, and they're going to find some of this money red-hot when they pick it up!

BUS

I wonder—

ALAN

You don't think it can be done—

BUS

I don't think you can do it.

ALAN

I've been on a crooked school board and I know how they jump for cover when you start looking at their books!

BUS

Well, it isn't exactly a school board.

ALAN

Oh, yes it is! Only a damn sight less intelligent! And they've all got weak spots! They can be had—and they're going to be—right on this bill they are! Why damn their goddamn eyes—

BUS

Mr. McClean, there's something about you that vaguely begins to appeal to me. Do you want any help?

ALAN

What kind?

BUS

I need a job. I was fired this morning. I know all
about everything. Have you got any plans?

ALAN

No, I haven't yet.

BUS

What of it? What I've forgotten is plenty for both
of us, and if we could include the setting off of a
few bombs, I'd find it a fascinating and congenial
occupation.

ALAN

Go on!

BUS

The House is split just about fifty-fifty on this bill.
A little finegling here and there, and a few promises,
and you might—yes sir, you might find yourself
with the deciding vote in your own little hands.

ALAN

I wouldn't know how to do that.

BUS

But I would. Oh, they made a foolish move today.
They left the Non-Partisans out of this bill. There
are four or five of 'em and they could swing Congress if they could stick in a lump for once. If we
could find— Beetles!

ALAN

What?

BUS

Beetles! The committee didn't give 'em their beetles, Mr. McClean.

ALAN

Oh, I begin to get you!

BUS

Of course you do. Now you go out and talk with a few Non-Partisans and you'll find yourself among friends.

ALAN

You think it will work?

BUS

I'm sure it will!

ALAN

Listen—you're hired!

BUS

Salary?

ALAN

Whatever it's been.
[*She puts out her hand. He takes it.*

BUS

Shall we go to lunch?

ALAN

Why not? I'm hollow.
[MERTON *enters from the office.*

MERTON

Oh, Mr. McClean, I wondered where you'd escaped to. I thought perhaps you'd like to lunch with me—

ALAN

What do you mean by escaped, Mr. Merton?

MERTON

Why—uh—we have several things to talk over—

ALAN

I rather doubt that. You're fired.

MERTON

Sir?

ALAN

I said, you're fired.

MERTON

I don't quite get it—

ALAN

Maybe you're a bit slow in the head. You're fired!

MERTON

But Mr. McClean! I've been secretary to the Congressmen from your district for many years now— if there's been any mistake made which I could rectify—

ALAN

You'd have to go back too far! You'd probably have to talk to your father and mother. You'd also have to make a lot of changes in your education and subsequent career. I said you're fired, and when I said

it, I meant it good and plenty! (*He turns to* BUS.)
Are you ready, Miss Nillson?

BUS

Hello, Merton!

CURTAIN

ACT TWO

ACT TWO

Scene I

Scene: The Office, three days later. Afternoon. MARJORIE *is at the desk.* SOL *enters with a letter in his hand, and looks at her morosely.*

SOL

Sons and heirs of boll-weevils and inch-worms. The lousy, filthy, air-polluting spoor of a mongrel dog. Did you hear what I said?

MARJORIE

What?

SOL

I said, those sons and heirs of a weak-minded seventh generation of boll-weevils and inch-worms—

MARJORIE

What's the matter, Sol?

SOL

Do you know what those quadruple asses have done?

MARJORIE

Who?

SOL .

The federal income tax bureau. They've disallowed enough exemptions over a period of four years to

77

soak me forty-five thousand dollars extra. Those
web-footed, ass-faced water-drinking, ossified de-
scendants of a bad smell. What have you got to be in
this carrion government to get your income tax
fixed? A Secretary of the Treasury?

MARJORIE

That helps. It helped before.

SOL

God, what a government! It's bad enough to have to
have it, but imagine having to pay for it! Tomorrow
I'm going to take a tin-cup and stand at the corner
of N Street and Pennsylvania Avenue. I'm going to
stand there with my hat off and a tin-cup in my
hand, asking alms from passers-by.

MARJORIE

You'd better take a jug along to go with the tin-
cup.

SOL

We're ruined, Marjorie, ruined. My real estate
equities are wiped out, the speakeasies are in the red,
the Playground's deserted, the bill isn't going to
pass, and I haven't got any more navy than Para-
guay.

MARJORIE

What do you mean, the bill won't pass? What's the
matter, Sol?

SOL

It's a rebellion. This McClean's a little David,
Marjorie, and he's got six strings on his harp, six
Farmer-Labor and Non-Partisan Leaguers lined up

with him to control the House and ride our bill to
destruction. And he'll do it, Marjorie, he'll do it!

MARJORIE

Oh, nonsense!

SOL

Wait and see. The old oracle's corns are hurting.

MARJORIE

How close is it?

SOL

We're dangling by a spider web, Clover. According
to my figures, there are eighteen members that could
go either way. The rest are pretty well nailed down,
for or against. Well, that eighteen has been talked to,
and the best I can make it, McClean's just one vote
behind. Let one more man swing over, and there'll
be a majority against us.

MARJORIE

Did Alan do all this?

SOL

He couldn't fail. We put the ammunition right into
his hands. And that's something for old Simeon Gray
to worry about.

MARJORIE

Sol, you've got to stop hammering at Dad. He's a
nervous wreck, and I'm worried about him. And you
do him no good!

SOL

I do him no good! What is he doing for me?

MARJORIE

What you don't get one way, you get another. (EDDIE *comes in from the hall*.) You're an artist at that, Sol—you know you are.

EDDIE

Hello, Sol! Say, Marjorie, could you do me a big favor?

MARJORIE

If it can be done quickly.

EDDIE

It's quite a job. That damn bill is lying in pieces all over my office.

SOL

Sure—they're sitting up nights slashing it to bits.

EDDIE

Miss Corey's been trying to paste it together, and confidentially, she's done one of the finest pasting jobs I've seen in years. If you help her for a few minutes you can name your price—

MARJORIE

I'll take a cigarette—but you'll have to wait till Dad gets here.

EDDIE

The committee meeting's in half an hour, remember. [LEVERING *and* WINGBLATT *enter*.

LEVERING

Eddie, I ought to take that flask of Sol's and hang a few glass medals on that glass brain of yours!

EDDIE

What's the matter?

LEVERING

I thought you were supposed to be watching McClean. What other use are you?

EDDIE

What's he done now?

WINGBLATT

Aren't we counting Trumper for one of our votes?

SOL

Yes—if he's still supposed to be sane.

WINGBLATT

Well, I happen to know he's been in McClean's office since one o'clock.
[MARJORIE *goes into the inner office.*

LEVERING

We lost two other votes this morning, and if he gets Trumper, he's over the line. I thought you said he was harmless!

EDDIE

Are you trying to make me the goat? I've done all I can! He got away from you too, didn't he? If this bill doesn't pass, I stand to lose a large amount of actual money.

WINGBLATT

And what kind of fake money do you think we stand to lose?

EDDIE

Well, I didn't put him on the committee, did I?

LEVERING

That's done with and let's not rake it up!

EDDIE

I suggest you'd better talk to Simeon.
[GRAY *enters from the hall.*

LEVERING

That's what I'm here for. He'll have to postpone
this meeting long enough to give us a chance to
attack those fellows one by one.

GRAY

Postpone the meeting? What for?

LEVERING

Because we may have to add something to that bill,
Sime, to push it through Congress.

GRAY

Add to it? Why?

SOL

A lot's been happening around here since we saw
you last! McClean's got Trumper in his office right
now, and if he brings him over we're one vote behind.

GRAY

What? Why you're crazy, Sol!

SOL

It's enough to drive a man crazy! Where have you
been?

GRAY

At the White House.

SOL

Hell, you've been there for two days now. What have you been doing? Taking lessons in smiling?

GRAY

We've been trying to cut down on this bill.

SOL

Cutting it down! If you don't start building it up pretty soon, this is going to be a purely imaginary bill, a mere wraith of legislation in all its functions and effects.

GRAY

Drop the oratory, Sol!

SOL

All right! But you'd better listen to me. I tell you this boy prodigy from Nevada is lifting every stone in Washington and tipping the worms off to their big chance. And they're turning, Sime, they're turning. Congratulate yourself!

GRAY

Me? Why didn't you go out after those Non-Partisans? You've handled 'em before.

SOL

It was you wouldn't give 'em that Japanese beetle patronage.

GRAY

McClean can't give it to them, either, can he?

SOL

I got down on my knees and begged you to let 'em have it! It's the first burning issue they've had since the Indian raids of '75. But you wouldn't give it to 'em. Now McClean's sold 'em on the idea that they can control the whole damn Congress if they stick together—and they're wild—there's no stopping them.

GRAY

I wish I'd known we were dealing with a maniac.

SOL

Why don't you give the bastards their beetles? You and the old man sitting up there and slicing off five dollars here and two ninety-eight there—

EDDIE

Sure, tell 'em they can have their beetles! What difference does it make?

GRAY

What do you think, Disraeli?

LEVERING

There's nothing else to do.

GRAY

All right. Go ahead.

WINGBLATT

If we want to do any more scouting before the committee meets, we'd better do it now! The whole damn Farmer-Labor geselshaft is in conference downstairs!

LEVERING

Let Sol tackle them, Wingie! You'd better go after Trumper!

WINGBLATT

But what can I promise him? Nobody's told me how far I can go—outside of the beetles!

GRAY

Do you need more than that?

LEVERING

If you do, let him have it!

WINGBLATT

And can he take it? Let's go.

GRAY

Sol, are you dead on your feet?

SOL

I don't think it'll do any good. They say even God has his price—but there's no arguing with these Scandinavians! Come on, Wingie.

[SOL *and* WINGBLATT *go out.*

LEVERING

You and the President may have to loosen up a bit on this bill, Sime.

GRAY

I wouldn't be too optimistic. We sat six solid hours over this thing today, and I give you my word, he won't stand for a dollar we don't need for the vote.

LEVERING

Yes, but a few more dollars may be needed, Sime!

In any case you'd better hold off your meeting till
we know where we are!

GRAY

Right!
[LEVERING *goes out.*

EDDIE

Forget about those Non-Partisans, Sime. We've got
more trouble than that!

GRAY

Yes? Where?

EDDIE

I just had a call from the cuttlefish. He's threatened
to withdraw his support, and you know what that'd
mean! the whole middle west against us! Why, we
wouldn't have a prayer. You know why, of course.

GRAY

No—why?

EDDIE

He's in with this Committee of 48 on National Defense.

GRAY

What's that got to do with it?

EDDIE

Well, National Defense, Simeon—

GRAY

The Committee of 48 on National Defense is another name for about 48 steel companies.

EDDIE

I didn't mention it before, Sime, because I figured on holding out on them for your sake. But I can't do it. They were sore about being left out of the omnibus bill, and they mean to get in on this or know the reason why.

GRAY

What do they want?

EDDIE

Rehabilitation of two battleships.

GRAY

Two battleships! That's fifteen millions!

EDDIE

Might be about that.

GRAY

Why, you're insane!

EDDIE

You don't know how this one interlocks—the steel crowd, the cuttlefish, the Pennsylvania machine, the aluminum boys—I can't fight 'em all.

GRAY

Tell 'em it can't be done.

EDDIE

They won't listen.

GRAY

Then let 'em wait. Why should they try to unload Navy stuff onto a deficiency bill?

EDDIE

They think it's a good spot.

GRAY

A battleship's no damn good any more—in peace or war—and they know it. And yet they spend fortunes to wreck disarmament conferences and keep the high seas cluttered with their antediluvian tin cans.

EDDIE

I know all that, Sime—but they're pinching me.

GRAY

You'll be re-elected, Eddie!

EDDIE

Not if I flop on this. They can pick their own man.

GRAY

I hate to refuse you, Eddie, but it's too much.

EDDIE

I'll have to have it, Simeon.

GRAY

It's impossible! If you can't get it, you can't—and that ends the argument.

EDDIE

Now listen, Simeon—everybody's in on this bill.

GRAY

Oh, no.

EDDIE

That river dredging scheme. Where does that come in—

GRAY

That's out. I saw the general.

EDDIE

Well, that Veterans' Bureau—what about that?

GRAY

Why pick on that? Do you expect me to fight the American Legion?

EDDIE

I suppose not. And there's that Massachusetts crowd—and that penitentiary at Culver—

GRAY

What?

EDDIE

That penitentiary at Culver— How did that get in there?

GRAY

It was put there in Committee—why?

EDDIE

By whom?
[*A pause.*

GRAY (*slowly*)

By me.

EDDIE

Why?

GRAY

What's wrong with it?

EDDIE

I'm asking you.

GRAY

Nothing.

EDDIE

I hear different. Who's the majority stock holder
of the Culver bank? Who knows that it's bound to
crash?

GRAY

So, it was you—

EDDIE

What?

GRAY

I thought McClean had been looking me up—it was
you.

EDDIE

You're wrong, Sime—

GRAY

Don't Sime me, God damn you! I thought you were
a friend of mine—

EDDIE

I am—anything I know about you I must have
heard in a perfectly open way.

GRAY

You had the Dahl Agency look up what I owned.

EDDIE

You're wrong, Sime—dead wrong!

GRAY

Don't lie to me! I made it my business to find out.

EDDIE

You were looked up, but not by me. Sprague had it done for the company.

GRAY

It comes to the same thing. You're Sprague's hired man!

EDDIE

Well, where do you get this stuff of walking around here as if you were God's favorite archangel dispensing favors in the lower regions! It's rather nice to know that you're just one of us after all!

GRAY

Would you expect me to publish a thing like that to the hyenas on the committee?

EDDIE

Well, what are you going to do about it?

GRAY

We haven't got a majority anyway and a couple of battleships ought to sink us cold—so put 'em in. Just to make sure we lose!

EDDIE

We certainly will lose if they aren't in. So what's my answer?

GRAY

You get your fifteen million! And you can take your

rake-off out of it—and you know what I think of you!

EDDIE

Well, I've been puzzled about you, Simeon—but not now.

GRAY

That all you want?

EDDIE

It'll do for the time being. No hard feelings?

GRAY

You think not!
[BUS *enters from the committee room.*

BUS

It's no business of mine, Eddie, but your Miss Corey is up to her eyebrows in mucilage and hysterics. She'll never untangle that bill in time—

EDDIE

Marjorie said she'd lend a hand—

GRAY

Marjorie's going to be busy.
[*He goes into the office.*

EDDIE

Give Miss Corey a lift with that copy, will you, Bus?

BUS

Sure—why not?

EDDIE

Thanks. Don't make it too permanent. There may be another change or two. (ALAN *enters from the hall.* Hello, McClean!

ALAN

How are you, Mr. Wister? (EDDIE *goes out.*) Oh, my God—Bus!

BUS

Well, I thought that confab with Trumper would never end. How did it come out?

ALAN

That man's crazy!

BUS

Don't say that. What did he want?

ALAN

Free seeds and free silver!

BUS

I don't believe it!

ALAN

It's true. He wants to flood the country with free silver.

BUS

Well—good Lord—give the country free silver. I say it ought to have free silver.

ALAN

It's not funny, Bus.

BUS

Well, give it free gasoline, then, and fiat money! We need Trumper's vote.

ALAN

You don't know what he's like!

BUS

Oh, yes, I do. He thinks he's the logical candidate for the next Presidential nomination.

ALAN

Exactly! He spent three-quarters of an hour reading me his speech of acceptance.

BUS

That was a short one—God, the ones I've heard of his. Is he still there?

ALAN

Yes.

BUS

Nobody with him?

ALAN

No, he's just sitting there!

BUS

Alan, this is our moment! Go back and talk to him— tell him you've been thinking things over—"Mr. Trumper, you're a great statesman, and I consider it a privilege to support you!"

ALAN

You don't know what I've let myself in for with the

rest of them to get the votes we've got! I've had to
pledge myself to an increased tariff on lumber and
an increased tariff on wheat, a new system of land-
banks, an embargo on circus animals—including
Siamese cats!

BUS

Cats?

ALAN

Cats!

BUS

Cats and beetles! Well, what of it? What we want is
to defeat this bill. You don't need to worry about
those promises, because you'll never be called on to
deliver. Why not one of them will even get out of
committee.

ALAN

But Bus—

BUS

We've done everything but give it the final push-over!
You're not going to fall down on that! What's a
promise or two—this is Washington!

ALAN

Bus, this is funny up to a point—but I simply will
not and cannot go near Trumper again. I can't
work this way.

BUS

Well, what are you going to do?

ALAN

I don't know, but I've got to think of someone else.

BUS

Why? Trumper's ideal—he's a jelly fish!

ALAN

But there's nothing ideal about the way you want me to get him. You've been swell, Bus—I couldn't have got started at all without you, but our methods turn my stomach over. They're just like everyone else's, and I'm calling a halt right now.

BUS

There is no other method in this place, Alan.

ALAN

God, what happens to people here?

BUS

You'll find out some day. You can't just go to a Congressman and say, "Please mister, vote on our side because it's honest!"

ALAN

I'm not quite that naive. But there must be a few here who see—as well as I do—that this regime is damn near over! There must be a few who're sick of the way things are being done and ready to take a chance for once.

BUS

For instance—who?

ALAN

Well—Sol, for one!

BUS

Sol!

ALAN

Yes, Sol! He knows it! And more than that he has a damn good reason to be sore right at the moment!

BUS

Alan, the strain's begun to tell on you!

ALAN

No, I've got to do this my way. It may seem crazy to you but it doesn't to me! I'm going to talk to him!

BUS

Alan, you're in for a terrible headache! I'd better go clean up after the efficient Miss Corey.
[SOL *enters from the hall.*

SOL

Hello! How's the opposition?

BUS

In beautiful shape, Sol—beautiful! You're wasting your time, Alan.
[*She goes into the committee room.*

SOL

Alan, that was a smooth piece of work, picking up Bussy the way you did—and I won't keep it from you, you've got us worried.

ALAN

I hope so, Sol.

SOL

I've got a proposition for you, Alan. Show me your
lists and you can see mine—all open and above board.
Because I'll tell you the truth, according to my
reckoning we've got you. That is, unless you've seen
somebody else I'm not figuring on—

ALAN

I've seen everybody!

SOL

Tell me one thing and I'll know the whole story.
Have you seen Trumper?

ALAN

Oh, yes, I've seen him.

SOL

And he came over to you?

ALAN

Well, he offered to.

SOL

Then I'm wrong. Sol's wrong again, and you're one
vote ahead. Is that the way you dope it?

ALAN

If I sell out for what he wants.

SOL

But you aren't going to do it? A man of your principles? You wouldn't trade back and forth like the
rest of us?

ALAN

Sol, I want to ask you something.

SOL

Anything, Alan, anything.

ALAN

You think we're enemies now—we're working against each other—and you don't trust me—but we're really on the same side.

SOL

Well, frankly, I didn't know I'd been playing into your hands to that extent.

ALAN

You remember what you said to me in the committee room, the first time I saw you? You said when you first came to Washington, you were young and a radical and the whole system made you sick—didn't you?

SOL

Did I say that?

ALAN

And it was true—wasn't it?

SOL

You aren't making an appeal to my virtue, Alan? My lost virtue?

ALAN

I'm saying that you know I'm right about this thing —and you're wrong.

SOL

There's a simple formula for deciding what's right
and wrong in politics, lad. It comes down to one
rule! God's always in the money. He don't lose.

ALAN

But suppose God's changed sides! The thing you'd
better start worrying about is that you're going to
wake up some morning and find yourself an old man
—and not only old, but out—down and out.

SOL

Why boy, you're eloquent! Only isn't it kind of a
last resort to come to old Sol and try to win him
over?

ALAN

You know this gang isn't going to last. They're
afraid—Gray's afraid and the President's afraid.
They feel that something's happened and something
has—something's snapped!

SOL

God, boy—you make me wonder. You shake me, Alan,
and I haven't been shaken for a long time. You think
the people are changing—waking up?

ALAN

I know they are.

SOL

Now it's been my firm conviction, fortified by thirty
years' experience, that the people don't change—and
they seldom or never wake up. In fact, I have found
no word in the English language and no simile or

figure of speech that would express the complete and illimitable ignorance and incompetence of the voting population. But maybe I don't go back far enough. Maybe it's a longer cycle than I take in.

ALAN

They're awake now—and they're going to throw you all out—all of you.

SOL

Wait a minute—wait till I pour myself a drink. (*He does so.*) Now, what do you want me to do?

ALAN

I want you to vote against the bill.

SOL

Give me reasons, Alan, give me reasons.

ALAN

You get nothing out of it, even if it passes, do you?

SOL

No. But if I voted against it I'd be out with all my friends.

ALAN

What of it? You and I could control the House now, Sol. We could wreck their machine, we could wreck their bill. Think of it—we could show them there are more honest men than thieves for once.

SOL

It ain't true though. There ain't half as many honest

men as thieves. Never have been. There's just one
fallacy in this argument of yours. Would it be your
plan, in case we get control, to run this government
honest—as being the best policy?

ALAN

Why not?

SOL

Then there wouldn't be anything in it for anybody,
would there? Nothing beyond his salary?

ALAN

Well—no.

SOL

You see, that's the fatal flaw!

ALAN

You want to come with me, Sol. You know you do.
And I'm counting on you.

SOL

You're counting on me! I'd better tell you about
myself, boy, before you say any more! Long ago
when I was slim and eagle-eyed, I had a good angel.
You wouldn't believe it to look at me now, but old
Sol had a good angel by his side back there in the
morning of time. And when a question like this came
up this angel of light would come shouldering round
him, arguing for righteousness, arguing against evil
courses and the selling of his soul. If I was going
to do wrong I had a wrestle with that angel. Like
Jacob of old I wrestled with him in the night, and
like Jacob of old I often came out ahead. It got so

that the angel didn't have a chance with me, Alan, and after a while he got tired. Temptation would come upon me and I'd look around for this here spirit to wrestle with, and he wouldn't be there. He ought to be here wrestling with me now, Alan, but he's quit me. He don't even brush his wings by me, let alone give me a struggle. So I'm just an old man soaked in tobacco and fusel oil, and no help to anybody. No, if it's up to me to stop the bill, it'll pass. You never get anywhere by taking things away from people, Alan. You've got to give them something.

ALAN

Why?

SOL

Because the sole business of government is graft, special privilege and corruption—with a by-product of order. They have to keep order or they can't make collections.

ALAN

Oh—oh, I see. Sol—

SOL

Don't say it, Alan, don't say it.

ALAN

Sol, you know—you may be right.

SOL

No, I'm all wrong. But what I'm mostly wrong about is I don't steal in a big enough way. Steal apples and they put you in jail—steal a nation and the hosts of heaven come down and line up under your banners.

ALAN

That's what I mean.

SOL

What?

ALAN

That's exactly what I mean!

SOL

I don't get you!

ALAN

I guess you're right, that's all. I guess you're right.

SOL

I'm right as far as I'm concerned. Sol's dyed in the wool—a black sheep—and whitewash won't cover him.

[WINGBLATT *enters from the hall.*

WINGBLATT

Sol, can you come out here a minute?

SOL

Good news, Wingie?

WINGBLATT

Not especially good news for McClean—but good news!

SOL

You haven't been promising things?

WINGBLATT

No—no! Just free seeds and free silver! God, the punishment I've been taking. Campaign speeches for Christ's sake!

SOL

That's better than having to make 'em!
[*They exit laughing.* ALAN *goes to the phone.*

ALAN

Get me Mr. Wister's office. Hello! Bus?—Alan! Are you where you can talk?—No, you were right about Sol. And they've grabbed Trumper too!—No, I'm not licked! But I've got another idea! No, no—I don't like what it means a damn bit. It's as rotten as every other method in this place, but it's the only chance I've got left. I want you to get copies of everything ever proposed for H.R. 2007.—I'm going to use my information—you know what.—Oh, God, Bus, I know that! I know it's a dirty thing to do! I have more reasons than you have for not liking it! But I've got to do it, and nobody's going to stop me! Oh, let's not talk about it! Just get me the copies of those things, and get 'em here quick!
[SOL *enters from the hall.*

SOL

Tact, boy, tact! Now you see, Alan, with a little tact and longsuffering, Wingie's just brought Trumper into camp—and we've got you licked. Has it ever occurred to you that you might be conducting your life on too high a moral plane?

ALAN

That's just what I have been thinking!

SOL

What?

ALAN

I guess your methods are better than mine, that's all. If I'm not on the inside I'll be out altogether.

SOL

Now, don't let me overpersuade you, Alan. You stick to your line.

ALAN

You don't want me on your side?

SOL

Good Lord! I wouldn't believe it for a minute.

ALAN

Well, you may when it happens. I'm going to ask for something in the bill myself.

SOL

You're going to ask for something? Don't do it, Alan.

ALAN

I'm going to ask for that extra million for Nevada irrigation.

SOL

And vote on our side?

ALAN

Yes.

SOL

But you're away late asking for it now, Alan. You should have put in your bid earlier.

ALAN

Don't you think I have a certain amount of influence—just for the moment?

SOL

Now, look here—was this whole set-up of yours a badger game? It's going to look that way.

ALAN

But what does it matter how it looks? Dell's in it—and Sneden and the veterans' lobby—and even Mr. Gray—

SOL

No—not Gray.

ALAN

I thought so. Isn't he? That prison at Culver's his, isn't it? I thought it was.

SOL

Oh, no, no, no! You're off the beat there. Simeon's never been hooked up with anything.

ALAN

But as I understand it, the bank's mainly his, and the money's badly needed—

SOL

As you understand it? Where did you hear this?

ALAN

It was an accident.

SOL

Oh, it was—

ALAN

But it's certain enough to get me anything I'd ask for. I wouldn't tell this to anyone else, Sol, but you're a friend of mine, and I know it won't get spread around.

SOL

Alan, you paralyze me. I get sober listening to you. Or am I sober? I take it you're not a drinking man?

ALAN

Not a heavy one!

SOL

Things like that don't come out by accident. You looked into it.

ALAN

Not intentionally. But you might as well have your fleet on the strength of it.

SOL

Boy, when I look at you and reflect on how I wasted my young time! The cunning of the serpent with the outward appearance of the dove! By God, I've never been up against it before!

ALAN

But Sol, if I'm going to make capital of it, you may as well do the same.

SOL

No. No, I can't use it on Simeon, Alan. You go in
and make your own deal. I'm not a man to take an
unfair advantage of a friend—never was a man to
do that.

ALAN

Well, don't use it if it's against your conscience.

SOL

No, no! I couldn't do it. Not to save my soul from
perdition! On the other hand—I ought to do it,
Alan. This generation that's growing up now, it's
a generation of vipers. You can't compete with 'em
without being a viper. Why, they're born with teeth
and claws nowadays. I'll just step in and see him a
minute.

ALAN

You really might as well.

SOL

Not about that. Just in a friendly way.

ALAN

Surely.

SOL

And I stood there telling you about my angel. An
old man's got to look out for himself. He's got to.
[*He goes into the office.* BUS *enters.*

BUS

Well?

ALAN

Are they complete copies?

BUS

Solid pork! What are you up to?

ALAN

I've been talking to Sol. He's in there getting his navy right now.

BUS

What?

ALAN

I'll catch the rest of them when the caucus meets, and advise them to ask for anything they want. They won't be refused.

BUS

What are you going to do?

ALAN

I'm going to overload the bill! I'm going to fill that thing with rubbish till no one will have the face to vote for it. Till it's a monstrosity and no one will dare sponsor it!

BUS

And this came to you all by yourself? Let me gaze on you, Alan. Let me contemplate the contours of that Nevada profile!

ALAN

Oh, you don't think it will work out?

BUS

On the contrary, I think it might. I think it will if you can carry it off. I resign, Alan. I abdicate. Take my hand and lead me. I'm a little child!

CURTAIN

ACT TWO

Scene II

Scene: The Committee Room.

MARJORIE *is taking the report.* DELL, SNEDEN, WINGBLATT *and* PEEBLES *are conversing.* MISS MCMURTY *is just entering through the hall door.* BUS *is just finishing putting papers together and looks up as* EDDIE *comes in from the office.*

BUS (*to* MARJORIE)

It's all here. You may find it a bit sticky.
[*She goes out to the office, closing the door.* EDDIE *picks up the sheaf and leafs it through.*

WINGBLATT

No—if we've got Trumper, he hasn't got a chance—look here.
[*He shows his figuring to* FARNUM.

PEEBLES

Was Trumper wobbling?

FARNUM

Good Lord, anyone can have Trumper that'll listen to him.
[GRAY *comes in from the office.*

GRAY

Have you got it together?

112

EDDIE

Seems to be all here. Six copies. I'm stepping out for a minute, Sime, but you can go ahead. I've okayed everything.
[*He goes out.*

WINGBLATT

Sime—where's Sol?

GRAY

I don't know. It doesn't matter. He's been over it with me.

SNEDEN

Is it going to pass, Simeon?

GRAY

So far as I know it is. Do you want to take a look at it?

SNEDEN

Sure.

MCMURTRY

Could I see a schedule of the accepted items?

GRAY

I beg your pardon. Certainly. (*He hands her the remaining copy.* ALAN *comes in and seats himself.*) Now, boys, I don't want this session to take too much time.

SNEDEN

Neither do I. This bill's ruining my game.

GRAY

Look them over and we can take the vote. We've been on the thing entirely too long.

FARNUM

Why should we spoil our day looking at it? It's all cut and dried anyway.

WINGBLATT

Put it in type, Simeon. There aren't any changes, are there?

GRAY

A few. I went over it with the President.

PEEBLES

One thing you can be sure of then—there's no good news in it.

MCMURTRY

I think the other members should be here.

DELL

Just for the hell of it?

GRAY

They will be. Look it over first, if you like.

DELL

Say, that veterans' hospital isn't eliminated, is it?

GRAY

It had to be, I saw Klein about that myself.

DELL

Well, what the hell!

PEEBLES

You can't do things this way, Sime. You've cut out that Iowa drainage.

GRAY

Had to do it—

FARNUM

Hey, boy—Sol got his navy.

GRAY

And Sol gets his navy. I had to admit it.

PEEBLES

You mean the President slashed that Iowa thing— and leased Sol the Atlantic Fleet?

GRAY

Right.

WINGBLATT

Sol got his Navy? Well, in that case—

SNEDEN

Look here, Sime—what's this "Naval rehabilitation"? Is that the fifteen million slice Eddie's been trying to get for his committee?

GRAY

That's it, and I couldn't avoid it. Those two, and the Japanese beetle, which we had to have for the Dakota vote, are the only items the committee hadn't concurred in.

WINGBLATT

Damn swell items, if you ask me.

PEEBLES

That's what I say. We're a long way over the budget.

GRAY

I don't like it any better than you do.

WINGBLATT

Well, why was it, then? The rest of us have had to surrender on one clause after another! You don't intend to rush this thing through without explaining?

GRAY

Not at all. If you want me to enumerate the reasons for every inclusion, it can be done. It'll take a lot of time, but—

DELL

We wouldn't be much ahead, Sime. But it certainly looks this time as if there were a few people on the inside who were getting what they wanted at the expense of the rest of us.

WINGBLATT

And personally I'm tired of taking one man's word for what we can have and what we can't! This caucus is supposed to be governed by majority vote—and by God, I think it should be!

GRAY

A fine mess you'd send over to the White House. [SOL and EDDIE enter.

FARNUM

I'd like to ask Sol there how he wangled that Navy out of you! I'd also like to ask Eddie why he's able to slip things in after the dead-line!

GRAY

If you wanted to influence this legislation you should have made a study of it.

WINGBLATT

I know—as you have.

GRAY

Yes, as I have. If you want this thing kicked back here—

SNEDEN

Oh what the hell! There's no use jawing with him. It's always this way. Let's get it over with.
[*He picks up his golf cap.*

ALAN (*rising*)

Mr. Chairman.

PEEBLES

Oh, let it ride!
[*He starts to rise.*

WINGBLATT

What do you say, Farnum?

FARNUM

What's the good? Let it go. I give up.
[*He gets up.*

ALAN

Mr. Chairman.
[*The committee is ready to go.*

GRAY

Mr. McClean?

ALAN

As you all know, I have been engaged, perhaps mistakenly, in attempting to defeat H.R. 2007. As matters stand now, it seems it will pass, and in the light of that knowledge I have been reconsidering a number of questions concerning it. I have gone over the Nevada project again—and I am convinced that, since the bill is to pass anyway, it would be wise to include the extra million for irrigation which was put over to next year.

MCMURTRY

An extra million! Well, I must say—

GRAY

You should have spoken earlier, Mr. McClean.

ALAN

Also, in looking over this project, I was drawn into a perusal of other items which have been offered for the bill and rejected—and with Miss Nillson's help I have made a list of all requests which were denied in preliminary discussions of the legislation. The list is long, longer, I believe, than the list of those accepted, but I have been amazed, and I think you will be amazed, to find that they are practically all measures of considerable value, calculated to relieve a great deal of unemployment—

SNEDEN

Are we going to finish up or not?

ALAN

Just one moment. I have copies of those rejected items. Would you care to look at the schedule?

GRAY

Thanks, I'm sufficiently familiar with them.

ALAN

Now, my point is simply this: these appear to me to be reasonable and justifiable proposals, quite as applicable to the present state of the country as any now incorporated. In consequence I am reversing my previous stand in the committee on this subject, and hereby move that this list, which I now offer, be added to H.R. 2007 in due form.
[*He hands up a sheaf of papers.*

DELL

Yeah?

PEEBLES

What's that?

GRAY

You're asking that all that junk go back in the bill?

ALAN

I am.

GRAY

I had enough grief getting it out and I have no intention of going through it again. The bill's in shape, and it's going to the house tomorrow just as it is.
[*He turns.*

ALAN

I'm making it as a motion, Mr. Chairman.

GRAY

Who put you up to this?

ALAN

> I'm acting on my own initiative. The plan originated with me.

GRAY

> You're welcome to it.

ALAN

> I shall be much obliged if someone will second my motion—

GRAY

> I'm entertaining no such nonsense—as a motion or anything else—

WINGBLATT

> What have you got here—everything that's been cut out of the bill?

ALAN

> Absolutely everything, I think.
> [*He goes about the room distributing copies.*

PEEBLES

> Let's see it.

DELL

> But what's the idea?

ALAN

> To put everything in that's been asked for.

DELL

> Everything?

ALAN

Why not? I find nothing unworthy of inclusion, and the decision rests with the majority.

FARNUM

Christ! That's Napoleonic!

WINGBLATT

You know, I'd be almost inclined to second that motion.

GRAY

I haven't recognized any motion.

SNEDEN

Is the veterans' administration in here?

FARNUM

My God, this one's got everything.

DELL

How about the uniforms for postal employees?

MCMURTRY

The appropriation for the nursing bureau—has it been included in this version?

WINGBLATT

God yes! All the infant industries are in it—including bastardy! I tell you it's all here, boys! If anything was ever complete, this is.

GRAY

Have you had enough of this tom-foolery?

PEEBLES

What's the total, Mr. McClean?

ALAN

Including everything, four hundred and seventy-five
millions.

SNEDEN

That's impossible. It's a lovely dream, but it's not
for us.

ALAN

It's not impossible! I give you my word, gentlemen,
that if you pass the motion Mr. Gray will do everything in his power to see that the bill is made law.
He's pledged himself to get this dam completed.

GRAY

Are you making promises for me, now?

EDDIE

What do you mean, McClean? You give your word?

GRAY

Can't you see what he's trying to do? He's trying to
hang enough junk on this thing to sink it!

ALAN

Pardon me, Mr. Gray—I'm merely trying to follow
your lead—when you included the navy and the steel
company—

SOL

Oh, you feathered serpent! That's what you were
doing!

GRAY

Are you setting up as an expert now?

ALAN

I hardly think, Mr. Gray, that you were functioning as an expert when you allowed those two items to be included.

GRAY

Oh, you don't?

ALAN

No, sir.

GRAY

Perhaps you consider this maniacal proposal of yours a constructive solution?

ALAN

I am not trying to be constructive, Mr. Chairman— merely logical.

SNEDEN

Wait a minute! You call a four hundred and seventy-five million dollar bill for a forty million dollar appropriation logical?

ALAN

Not at all. I only say that if it is logical to include Mr. Wister's rehabilitated battleships on this bill, it is just as logical to include your veterans' administration.

SNEDEN

Well, that sounds reasonable.

SOL

Boys—he's slipping something over on you!

FARNUM

We've had plenty slipped over on us! The Atlantic Fleet for one thing!

GRAY

We're not including what we like here—we're including what we have to for the vote—and that's all!

PEEBLES

Well, suppose you had to include something useful— just had to? Certainly draining those Iowa swamps is at least a thousand times more sensible than appropriating good money to drag that fleet over to Sol's front yard—I leave it to the conference!

GRAY

There's a tremendous difference in the amounts.

ALAN

Exactly eight thousand five hundred dollars—to be precise.

EDDIE

And that's important information too.

PEEBLES

My God, is that all?

MCMURTRY

Well, surely there's considerable difference between fifteen thousand dollars appropriated to provide nurses for the poor—and fifteen million to repair two battleships!

EDDIE

If you imbeciles don't recognize this thing as the most obvious damned trick in the world—Christ! I'd have drawn up the bill myself without bothering—

WINGBLATT

It looks like you did anyway. What I still want to know is—

GRAY

Ask it later! Are we going to settle this bill or not? It's got to go to the House tomorrow and McClean comes in here with a Civil War grandstand play and sets you by the ears!

ALAN

I assure you that was not my intention, Mr. Chairman.

GRAY

Will someone please make a motion to put this bill to a vote so we can get out of here?

ALAN

I move that the bill is unanimously accepted—with all items, clauses and appropriations which I have included—

GRAY

I don't know whether you're insane or you've been put up to it. Will someone move to put this bill to a vote?

SOL

I so move.

EDDIE

I second the motion.

WINGBLATT

Now, wait a minute, Simeon! Don't pull a fast one on us. I still want to get to the bottom of how and why Sol got his fleet.

FARNUM

Yeah! And I still want to know why Eddie was allowed to push his steel company in after the deadline! What about that?

GRAY

The President agreed—at the urging of the Committee of 48 on National Defense—

DELL

My God, is the cuttlefish super-chairman of this committee too?

EDDIE

He was certainly going to swing the whole Middle West against us if we didn't do something for the Committee of 48!

WINGBLATT

Says you! I second Mr. McClean's motion!

GRAY

For God's sake, Wingie!

EDDIE

There's a motion before the committee, unless I'm wrong.

MCMURTRY

I hardly see why the rest of us should be put aside
to accommodate Mr. Wister and Mr. Fitzmaurice.
If the Chairman found it necessary to trade for votes
there are others on the committee who might have
had votes to offer!

SOL (*muttering*)

Angels! Jacob of Old! You double-crossing little—

SNEDEN

Certainly. Why didn't you let us in on it, and give
us a chance?

MCMURTRY

Doesn't the President consider uncared for babies an
item in national defense?
[*She snorts.*

GRAY

Why don't you address all these questions to Mr.
McClean?

ALAN

Mr. Chairman—

GRAY

Are you trying to filibuster the whole damn day
away! Now I ask you again to bring it to a vote.

WINGBLATT

All right! Let McClean talk!

PEEBLES

What did Sol have up his sleeve, Mr. McClean?

ALAN

Since, as Mr. Gray reminds us, there is already a question before the committee, I call for that question. Let us first vote on the bill without the additions—

WINGBLATT

And that's an idea, too. Question.

GRAY

If you are under the impression that we can make decisions of this character in any off-hand and childish spirit—

WINGBLATT

We know all that—and you've been asking for a vote! Well, put it!

PEEBLES

Sure, question!

SEVERAL

Question!

GRAY

Very well. Those in favor of sending 2007 to the House as it stands—

EDDIE AND SOL

Aye.

GRAY

Opposed.

REST OF THE COMMITTEE

No.

WINGBLATT

I guess that's fairly obvious.

GRAY

And now, having reached what is probably a new low for all time in common-sense, I suggest that we adjourn till tomorrow.

EDDIE

I move we adjourn.

ALAN

I made a motion a little while ago which was not recognized, Mr. Chairman—a motion for the inclusion of the items in this copy of the bill. I wish to offer that motion again.

WINGBLATT

And I wish to second it!

GRAY

Not today.

WINGBLATT

Yes, today!

SNEDEN

You can't adjourn the meeting!

FARNUM

Personally, I'd like to vote on McClean's motion, and before I do I'd like to hear McClean's reason why Sol and Eddie can get away with murder.

PEEBLES

So would I. And we're not leaving till we find out. I

want to hear the rest of the story. (*To* ALAN.) Go ahead and talk.

ALAN (*his eye on* GRAY)

I don't see that any explanations are needed. Ask for what you want, and you'll get it, that's all.

GRAY

If Mr. McClean will pardon me, I'll do a little talking myself about his inspired suggestion. It's obvious that he has nothing in mind except to make this bill look like a raid on the treasury. You all know my position in such matters. I am the one man among you who has given his time to government finances over a period of years. I've carried the work and made the decisions because I know what can and what cannot be done. Now McClean has come in here with the deliberate intention of stampeding you into a log-rolling vote that will look like an organized steal, and he thinks he can get away with it—and he thinks I don't dare say anything because he's discovered that I have stock in a bank at Culver, and Culver is affected by one of the allottments in this bill. That's his whole case. If that gives him status as an expert and puts him in control here, why pass his resolution. If you still trust my judgment or think my word's any good, you'll send the measure to the House as it stands.

[*A pause.*

PEEBLES

How much stock do you hold in the Culver bank, Mr. Chairman?

GRAY

A third interest. Anything else?

PEEBLES

No. Not from this side—
[*A pause.*

GRAY

Now, I should like to call for another vote on the bill as it stands.

FARNUM

Does that mean including Sol and Eddie?

GRAY

It does.

SNEDEN

They get what they're asking for?

GRAY

They do.

SNEDEN

Then I don't see why we shouldn't.

WINGBLATT

Nor I. How come, Simeon?

GRAY

Those items have been accepted—

SNEDEN

How much more will the bill stand?

GRAY

It won't stand a nickle.

WINGBLATT

In other words—just because a couple of guys got
in under the wire with this information—they're
the white-headed boys.

GRAY

The bill is carrying every possible cent it can. What's
more, it'll absolutely be vetoed if you add anything
to it—anything.

PEEBLES

I don't quite believe that. As a matter of fact, boys,
I don't believe that at all. It won't be vetoed.

GRAY

All right, hang yourselves.

WINGBLATT

We've been rooked by an inside gang—that's what's
happened.

FARNUM

And now they're trying to tell us the House won't
pass it and the Old Man'll veto it if we ask for what
they got.

SNEDEN

Why, this bill's all set to pass, and the President's
all set to sign it.

WINGBLATT

I seconded a motion here a minute ago!

PEEBLES

What's that steel business but highway robbery?

WINGBLATT

That's all! I call for the question.

FARNUM

Question!

PEEBLES

And what happens? Nothing—except the bill carries more than expected. Sure— Question!

GRAY

Dell?

DELL

There's nothing in here I could object to, Simeon.

GRAY

Very well. All in favor of including the items in Mr. McClean's list will signify by saying aye.

THE COMMITTEE (*except* SOL, EDDIE *and* GRAY)

Aye.

GRAY

The motion is carried. Adjourned.
[*There is silence, the members begin to stir.*

MCMURTRY

I'm afraid we've done a most appalling thing. Shouldn't we reconsider?

PEEBLES

We should not.
[SOL *rises.*

FARNUM

It's all right, Sol. You're getting yours too.

SOL

Nobody's getting anything if you ask me! Imagine
me trusting a missionary! And at my age! Angels!
[SOL *and* EDDIE *go out.*

FARNUM

Listen, Sneden—keep this away from the reporters
tonight. Keep it dark till it's read.

SNEDEN

Yeah! That's a thought, too.

MCMURTRY

I'm sure we've done a most appalling thing.
[*They go out.* ALAN, MARJORIE *and* GRAY *are alone.*
ALAN *goes toward the door.*

GRAY

Just a moment, Mr. McClean. You've beaten me here
this afternoon, and made a good job of it. No doubt
it looks to you as if no man with a remnant of honesty would have the face to present the thing to the
House.

ALAN

Yes, that is the way I feel, Mr. Gray.

GRAY

That is one way of looking at it, McClean. But you
once told us about a little town where the people had
no money to buy. I want to tell you about another
town. I grew up in Culver and I know the people
there—the storekeepers and the professional men
and the people in the street. I know them by their

first names—and I know what they've been through. They've lost nearly everything they had. Business is gone and two banks have failed. The third one's mine, and people think it's sound, and what money is left is in it. But the bank isn't sound; and if the bill's defeated and the penitentiary doesn't go to Culver, the bank will fail, and a lot of people will lose their life savings and their jobs.

ALAN

But, Mr. Gray, isn't it a little unfair to support Culver by taxing other places which are just as badly off?

GRAY

Yes, it is unfair! But I'm here to represent a certain district, McClean, and they need what I can do for them as they've never needed it before. I don't hold what you've done against you, but I am going to fight you. I'm going to fight you every inch of the way. You've made it damn difficult! You've dumped 275 extra millions on the bill, and you expect that to kill it in the House. But I don't intend to let that kill it. This fight hasn't even begun. I'm not asking you to call off your dogs, and I'm not apologizing. I'm going to use every weapon I can lay my hands on, and I won't be very squeamish where or how I find them.

ALAN

You don't leave me much choice, do you?

GRAY

And you leave me no choice!

ALAN

That's going to make it very interesting!
[*He goes out.*

MARJORIE

Dad, what is it?

GRAY

Nothing!

MARJORIE

If you'd wanted to make him believe the worst possible about you— What does it mean? Why do you
want that bill to pass as much as all that?

GRAY

It's nothing that concerns you, Marjorie.

MARJORIE

It does concern me. If I didn't believe in you right
now, more than anything in the world, I'd be with
Alan against you.

GRAY

Perhaps you should be!

MARJORIE

It isn't fair to tell me just that much! I want an
answer! You must give me an answer!

GRAY

The third national bank of Culver is not merely in
difficulties, Marjorie. It has borrowed twice on federal securities. In its vaults are three packages of
bonds which, if examined, would prove to be blank

paper. If the bank fails those securities will be examined at once. I am chairman of the board. I was away when it was done, but I've known of it for some time! To put it baldly, I'm guilty. So you see, if I don't get my penitentiary one way, I'll get it another! Does that answer your question?

CURTAIN

ACT THREE

ACT THREE

Scene I

Scene: The Committee Room. Evening. Three days later. SNEDEN *and* DELL *are seated at the table.* PEEBLES *is near the door, having just entered to make a report, and* WINGBLATT *is standing at the small table.*

WINGBLATT

Do you mean to tell me you spent three hours with that Rhode Island bunch and couldn't even get a rise out of them?

PEEBLES

They said they'd vote for it if it looked like it was going through—

WINGBLATT

Well, good God, what good's that going to do?

PEEBLES

I haven't had any sleep for two nights, Wingie!

WINGBLATT

You go back there and tell them it is going through and quit boasting about the late hours you keep! Nobody's had any sleep as far as I know. Did you tell 'em about that federal base at Newport?

PEEBLES

I did. They're scared of it.

WINGBLATT

Scared of federal money? Don't make me laugh.

DELL

The President's bringing pressure, Wingie.

WINGBLATT

What kind of pressure?

DELL

Patronage pressure.

WINGBLATT

So that's it. That's why we keep losing votes as fast as we bring 'em in.

DELL

Sure it is. He wants it sent back to the committee and scaled down.

PEEBLES

And that's what's going to happen.

SNEDEN

It is not. We've had twenty thousand telegrams favoring this bill the last two days!

DELL

Yeah, but listen to this. Editorial in the Washington Tribune: "The plunderbund at the Capitol is over-reaching itself. One more big grab—"

WINGBLATT

That's an administration organ, that sheet. Plays any tune the President sets for it!

DELL

You won't find many papers don't say the same thing, no matter what their politics are.

WINGBLATT

Are you going haywire on us?

DELL

I don't want to be spanked in public, Wingie. I'd rather take my licking in the solitude of my own boudoir.

PEEBLES

You sure Dizzie's meeting us here?

DELL

That's what he said.

WINGBLATT

Who's been working on that Massachusetts crowd?

DELL

Farnum. They're all right! They'll be for it on account of the new lighthouse and harbor work.

WINGBLATT

That puts us four votes ahead.

SNEDEN

And then add in Illinois and it puts us four votes behind.

DELL

That's right.

PEEBLES

All I know is if this bill don't pass, I don't come

back here no more, and I haven't even got enough
left to buy me a hunting and fishing license.

DELL

What would a poacher like you want with a hunting
and fishing license?
[*The telephone rings.*

WINGBLATT

Damn it, they'll be calling the roll within an hour
and we don't know anything—we don't even know
how we're going to vote.

SNEDEN (*at the phone*)

Yeah. Well, why not? Eddie's supposed to handle
Delaware, isn't he? I don't know what more they
could ask for. All right, Dave.
[*He hangs up.* MARJORIE *enters from the office.*

MARJORIE

Where's Sol?

DELL

Downstairs, Marjorie. The manufacturing states
are holding a conference, and he's down there with
Farnum and Eddie.

MARJORIE

Dad just got a call from the Speaker. He says he
can't keep the debate going more than half an hour
longer. He'll have to let it come to a vote.
[*She goes out.*

WINGBLATT

Anything we want to do we better do right now.
[LEVERING *enters.*

LEVERING

Hello, boys.

SNEDEN

There he is.

WINGBLATT

Dizzy, for God's sake come in here and give us a
line on what's going to happen. These babes in the
wood think we're going to have to oppose our own
bill.
[MARK *opens the hall door and brings in a large
sack of telegrams.*

LEVERING

They may be right.

WINGBLATT

But why? Every organization in the country wants
it.

MARK

More telegrams, gentlemen.
[*He goes out.*

WINGBLATT

Look at what Mark's just brought in. And look at
those telegrams. Open any one of them! The country's screaming its head off for the thing!

LEVERING

Not the country. Don't confuse the country with the
people that still have money left to send telegrams.
They represent a very small fraction of the country.

DELL

He's right.

WINGBLATT

Everybody stands to benefit! Every state in the Union!
[EBNER *enters from the hall.*

EBNER

McClean isn't around here, is he?

SNEDEN

No, haven't seen McClean.

EBNER

Sorry, just looking for him.

WINGBLATT

Listen, Joe, while you're here will you tell me one thing?

EBNER

Sure!

WINGBLATT

What's got into this little Jesus McClean that makes you guys stick to him?

EBNER

He certainly put it over on you, Wingie.

WINGBLATT

Well, what are you radicals fighting us for? You've got clauses in that bill!

SNEDEN

You're just cutting your own throats voting against it.

EBNER

We don't want those clauses. You're in a hole, you boys, and McClean put you there, and we're going to keep you there. Personally I think you never will get out of it—and I think we'll blow this government higher than a kite before you know what's happened to you! I guess you never heard of a revolution, did you? Well, you're going to hear of one. And you can write that on your list, or print it on the wall, or put it up in lights over the Capitol!

[*He goes out.*

WINGBLATT

Gone Bolshevik, have they? Well, they won't get far with that.

SNEDEN

He's been reading the life of Trotzky in two volumes.

DELL

They've got an organization now, boys. They think this McClean's a new Bob LaFollette.

LEVERING

Unless we can make sure of a decisive majority for the bill, we'll all have to throw our weight against it. If we offend the country once more—

PEEBLES

Now don't say that, Dizzy. Don't say that.

LEVERING

It's out of my hands!

SOL (*outside*)

> And how can man die better
> Than facing fearful odds
> For the ashes of his fathers
> And the altars of his gods?

(SOL *enters.* MARJORIE *comes in from the office.*)
Dizzy, I've been out gathering recruits to stand at
my right hand and keep the bridge with me!

WINGBLATT

What's the news, Sol?

SNEDEN

How do we rate, Sol?

DELL

Oh, Sol, what was that Rhode Island business?

LEVERING

Let's have it, Sol. How did you come out?

MARJORIE

Sol, what happened?

SOL

Well, Clover, the situation called for a good deal of
oratory!
[FARNUM *and* EDDIE *enter.*

FARNUM

Oratory! What do you say to Pennsylvania!

MARJORIE

What do you mean? Did they come over?

EDDIE

What do you say to Indiana and Illinois?

FARNUM

What do you say to that vast and glorious Empire
State—New York to you!

WINGBLATT

Cut the comedy!

EDDIE

They came over!

FARNUM

Sol brought 'em over!

MARJORIE

We've got a majority?

FARNUM

A majority? We've got the damnedest, sweetest, most
beautiful majority I ever saw delivered in one pack-
age!
[MARJORIE *runs out*.

EDDIE

The whole blatting conference voted to go for it
solid!

SNEDEN

The rosy-fingered dawn appears!

LEVERING

That's Sol's work?

EDDIE

Sol's work!

FARNUM

And beautiful!

LEVERING

What did you do to 'em, Sol?

SOL

I talked to 'em. Where are appropriations supposed to originate in the government of the United States? In the House of Representatives. Then by what right does the President try to dictate how much we can appropriate, or where, or how? That's all.

DELL

What did you do? Give 'em your word of honor?

SOL

Honor? Pennsylvania gets twenty-one millions. Illinois gets those Lake Michigan docks—

SNEDEN

How can you promise docks on Lake Michigan?

WINGBLATT

Yeah, who gave you authority to do that?

SOL

It's in the bill!

DELL

Sure. Don't you remember?

SNEDEN

No, I do not. And I'll never believe it.

SOL

This is an extraordinary bill! It will keep a million people out of bread lines!

LEVERING

If it isn't vetoed.
[GRAY *and* MARJORIE *enter from the office.*

GRAY

Well, I hear we've got a majority!

DELL

We certainly have!

WINGBLATT

What's the news from the White House, Sime?

GRAY

Well, no news is good news, I suppose. So far he hasn't said a word. Collier promised to let me know if there was any decision.
[*The buzzer sounds twice.*

DELL

There goes the buzzer. Half an hour, Disraeli! How do we vote?

WINGBLATT

My God, is there any question any more? To hell with the country. We're climbing on the bandwagon!

FARNUM

Come on, Dizzy, don't hold up the procession.

PEEBLES

How about it?

LEVERING

How much of a majority have we got?

DELL

Fifty-five or sixty to the good!

LEVERING

We're breaking with the President, Sime!

GRAY

With that majority it's an act of God. He can't blame us for going along.

LEVERING

O.K., boys, we're voting "Aye."

DELL

Right.
[*There is a general sigh of relief. The crowd goes out through the hall door.* SOL, MARJORIE *and* GRAY *are left alone.*

SOL

Well, Sime, we're riding high.

MARJORIE

Sol, you're a genius!

SOL

I had to be!
[*The telephone rings.*

GRAY

You deserve your fleet—can I get you the Army for next summer?

SOL

Certainly, and you can throw in the Marines!

MARJORIE

Hello! What? Oh, just a minute. It's for you, Dad.

GRAY

Oh!
[*He goes to the phone.*

SOL

A wee nip, Clover? Just to celebrate?

MARJORIE

Why not?

GRAY

Hello!—Hello, Collier! What?—What!—You heard him say that? (SOL *and* MARJORIE *stop.*) Then it's definite—I see!—All right, thanks, Collier.—The President's decided to veto the measure if it passes.

MARJORIE

Where does that leave us, Sol?
[SOL *sits down to figure.*

SOL

About twelve votes shy of a two-thirds majority.

MARJORIE

We've got to get them, Sol. We've got to!

GRAY

There's never quite enough time, is there?

SOL

If I had an hour more, I might be able to fetch in those Californians.

GRAY

But there is less than half an hour, Sol.

MARJORIE

It can't go this way. Sol, you know what this means —it just can't happen.

GRAY

Maybe there's no way out of it.

MARJORIE

There must be—it takes so little to make them go one way or another.

SOL

It's so close right now, that if Alan was to forget his principles, we'd have our two-thirds and could beat the veto.

MARJORIE

Then something can still be done!

SOL

That's what I was thinking. Sime, are you going to mind if I put the case to him?

GRAY

I wouldn't do it, Sol—I'd rather nobody did it. I have some messages to send off.

SOL

Have it your own way, Sime. I think it's worth trying.

GRAY

Well, I don't. Nobody could deliver fifteen men in
the time that's left. And that being the case, I'd
rather you didn't mention the subject. I don't par-
ticularly like the idea of people feeling sorry for me.

SOL

I get you.
[GRAY *goes into the office.*

MARJORIE

How many votes are there in that group of Alan's?

SOL

About twenty under his wing—more than enough.

MARJORIE

Then I am going down to his office and get him. But
Sol, you will have to talk to him—this is something
I can't ask him, but you can.

SOL

I'm going to.

MARJORIE

I wish it were anybody else.

SOL

I'm glad it isn't anybody else.
[MARK *enters with a cup of coffee, sugar, paper nap-
kins and crackers.*

MARK

Oh! Excuse me!

MARJORIE

I'll be right back.
[*She goes out.*

MARK

I brought your coffee, sir.

SOL

Leave it there, Mark.

MARK

And Mr. Fitzmaurice?

SOL

Yes.

MARK

Do you know anything about this here money bill the papers is talking about? Taking all that money out of the Treasury?

SOL

I've heard about it, Mark.

MARK

Well, I was hoping you would be against that bill.

SOL

Why, boy?

MARK

Because this government's costing a sight too much. A sight!

SOL

I'd hate to see you go, Mark. But if you can stand it—

MARK

Me!

SOL

Don't you know the service in this building will be cut in half if the deficiency bill don't pass?

MARK

No, sir! I didn't know that. I certainly didn't. Maybe I spoke out of turn, Mr. Fitzmaurice!

SOL

Now it's high-minded of you to consider the good of the country.

MARK

I ain't really high-minded, Mr. Fitzmaurice. I ain't high-minded at all. No— I was just swayed by reading matter.

SOL

You aren't really against it?

MARK

On the whole, I ain't really against it at all. I'm really for it on the whole. I want to drop the whole matter, Mr. Fitzmaurice.
[BUS *enters from the office.*

SOL

Fine—we'll drop it. 'Evening, Bussy!

BUS

'Evening, Sol. How's the opposition tonight?

SOL

Well, Bussy— We view our prospects with a certain amount of optimism. I think we can safely say that.

BUS

Sounds like a brokerage firm with its back to the wall. How's Atlantic Fleet common?

SOL

You're dancing on the grave of an old man, Bussy.

BUS

You do look a bit low.

SOL

Not as low as I was this afternoon, though. We've taken over four manufacturing states from you since then.

BUS

What!

SOL

It's true—we're too far ahead to catch now.

BUS

That's a jolt! I might as well admit that jolts me pretty hard—if true!

SOL

How's the middle western bloc?

BUS

Oh, that's holding together in great shape. You weren't thinking of going after our farmers, Sol?

SOL

We're going to be too many for you on the vote, Bussy. So why hold out? Why not fall in line and get some of the credit?

BUS

Baby! Do you know what I think?

SOL

No.

BUS

By your tone of voice I think you're expecting a veto!

SOL

Serpent of Eden—I am!

BUS

And we can still hold you up?

SOL

That's the situation.

BUS

Then of course we will!
[ALAN *enters with* MARJORIE.

ALAN

Hello, Sol!

BUS

Alan, there's news! The President's going to veto the bill and that's our winning card!

ALAN

Great, Bus! Marjorie said you wanted to see me, Sol.

SOL

Alan, we're going over there to vote in about five minutes and I want you to do something for me.

ALAN

What is it?

SOL

I want you to release that middle western bloc of yours.

ALAN

Give me reasons, Sol—give me reasons!

BUS

Now what makes you think you'll get any help from us?

SOL

From Alan!

BUS

You have an eminent nerve! We may be just beginners, Sol; we may be putty in your hands, but we know better than that.

SOL

Alan, you're going to wish you had. Sometime you

are going to wish as you've never wished anything before.

BUS

Threats?

SOL

No, not threats. But you've got some people in a jam, Alan, and I can't get them out of it. Houdini couldn't get them out of it, but with your influence I think maybe you could.

ALAN

Who?

SOL

Simeon.

ALAN

I'm sorry, Sol, but I don't see why you come to me about this.

SOL

I only want to say one thing—you won't reform anything by defeating this one bill. Parties may come and parties may go—administrations come in and go out, but the graft varies only in amount, not in kind. Now you can defeat this one appropriation bill, just for your own noble satisfaction, but you won't reform anything, and it might be more to the point to be human—this once. I had a share in it, Alan, I helped you wreck him. Neither one of us knew what we were doing, but by God, we ought to do what we can to take it back.

ALAN

Just what do you mean by wreck, Sol?

SOL

I mean something you won't rest easy knowing, Alan.
I mean a term in jail.

ALAN

What?

SOL

I mean just what I said.
[EBNER *enters from the hall.*

EBNER

Oh, good evening. We're all waiting for you downstairs, McClean. Thought we'd go over in a body.

ALAN

Just a minute, Joe!

EBNER

And before we go down—one or two of the boys are
wavering a bit. It's hard for some people to turn
down patronage when it's offered on a platter. So it
might be a good idea to stick close to them. I'll do
what I can, and I'll expect you to back me up.

BUS

Run along, Joe, Alan will catch you downstairs.

EBNER

We'll go down in history! This is the day the Old
Guard meets its Waterloo!

ALAN

Give me three minutes, will you, Joe?

EBNER

Say, you aren't letting yourself be talked to?

ALAN

No. I'll be with you in a minute—but for God's sake, get out now! Marjorie, is it true?
[EBNER *goes out.*

MARJORIE

Yes. I don't know whether you will ever forgive me or not, Alan. I'm going back on everything I believed, but things look different when there is a prison staring someone in the face. I don't care any more whether it's honest or not. I don't want him to go through with it.

ALAN

But what has your father done?

MARJORIE

I've loved him and almost worshipped him—because he was honest and just, and they couldn't corrupt him—somebody had to be honest in this place, or you couldn't breathe the air—and he isn't really guilty even now.

ALAN

Guilty of what, Marjorie?

MARJORIE

Something at the bank, Alan. Some misuse of funds

that he wasn't concerned in at all. Only it falls on
him.
[The buzzer sounds twice.

ALAN

I'm afraid it's impossible—even if there were time.

SOL

There must be two or three key men, Alan, who could
bring the others around if you worked with them.

ALAN

Worked with them? Go to those farmers and ask them
to vote for the bill, after what I've done to it?

BUS

We've wasted a week's work, Alan. You'd better turn
those votes loose.

SOL

We're counting on you!
[The buzzer sounds three times.

ALAN

Counting on me! Why, I couldn't find words to say it
to them. I'm sorry, Marjorie, but I can't think of
any one person now. I'm not fighting you or your
father. I'm fighting this machine!

MARJORIE

But think what it means to him!

ALAN

I hope you're wrong about it and the blame doesn't
fall on him, but even if it does, I can't stop now. If
I were wiser, I might know how to compromise. I may

be sending an innocent man to prison and I wish to
Christ I knew how to avoid it, but I don't!
[*The buzzer sounds four times.*

MARJORIE

   Alan! Alan!

ALAN

   Don't ask it of me and don't tell me what I've lost!
   I know what I've lost from all of you. And it's not my
   choice to lose it—but I'm in a fight that's got to be
   won—and you're asking for something I've no right
   to give!

                   CURTAIN

ACT THREE

Scene II

Scene: The Committee Room. Later the same evening.

SNEDEN, FARNUM, PEEBLES, WINGBLATT, EDDIE, SOL *and* DELL *appear in the doorway singing:*

THE CROWD

> Take it away, my boys—take it away!
> When we get started everybody has to pay,
> Pay, pay, pay!   •
> Take it away, my boys—take it away!
> We hear the eagle screaming:
> Pht the army! Pht the navy! Hey!

PEEBLES

Who said "Pht the army"? Who said that?

SNEDEN

Good old Peebles! Peebles is in the R.O.T.C. A lieutenant, by God!

PEEBLES

Do you realize you're talking to a son of the American Revolution?

WINGBLATT

A son of what?

DELL

I'm not a drinking man—but I'm drinking.

WINGBLATT

Shut up, will you? I want to know what Peebles is a son of?

CROWD (*singing*)

Take it away, my boys—take it away!
Mama loves papa almost every other day,
Day, day, day!
Take it away, my boys—salt it in brine!
Please pass the bacon, Elmer!
Pht the people, pht the people, hey!

FARNUM

Well, boys—who won?

THE CROWD

We did!

FARNUM

Who lost?

THE CROWD

Nobody!

SOL

Have you all got your bribes? Everybody satisfied? Hold up your hands, them that didn't get their bribes!

PEEBLES

Bribes! Bribes! Sir, I don't care for your choice of words.

WINGBLATT

Yes, suh! We both resent that, suh! As professional Southerners, we resent that! You'll take that back, suh, and you'll couch it in less invidious terms, suh!

SOL

How's times, boys? Everybody prosperous? Everybody flying high?

WINGBLATT

Oh yes, suh, massah! Everybody prosperous.

SOL

Corn in the crib and sorghum in the barrel?

WINGBLATT

Oh yes suh, massah! Corn in de crib and sorghum in de barrel!

SOL

And how-all's Miss Meadows and the gals? Sitting pretty on the front porch, I take oath. Eating pork?

WINGBLATT

Um-um, massah!

SOL

And riding horses, plenty of riding horses for a gentleman?

WINGBLATT

Massah, did you-all say riding horses?
[BUS *enters from the office.*

BUS

Have you all gone crazy? What happened?

SEVERAL

They passed the bill!

BUS

One at a time—what?

SOL

They passed the bill!

BUS

Well, what of it? It's going to be vetoed, anyway.

WINGBLATT

Good God, it passed with a two-thirds majority—
and it can't be vetoed!
[MARJORIE *enters from the office.*

BUS

Alan released those votes!

SOL

He didn't! His farmers stuck together. But they
weren't enough—not near enough!

MARJORIE

How much of a majority was there?

SOL

It was a landslide! Maybe fifteen or twenty stood out
against it!

MARJORIE

Then—it's certain.

WINGBLATT

Certain! The whole House went crazy!

FARNUM

It looked like the Klondike gold rush!

MARJORIE

Has Dad come back yet?
[*She goes into the office.*

SOL

It was Alan who did it, Bus, and we're giving him credit for it!

BUS

He'll like that a lot.
[ALAN *enters from the hall.*

SOL

Alan, my boy, I've been appointed by this delegation to tender you a little message. Tonight you feast at our expense with sparkling burgundy and venison pie.

ALAN

No thanks, Sol. Is Marjorie in the office, Bus?

BUS

Yes, Alan.

SOL

Boy, it was a stunning job!

WINGBLATT

It's a system!

SOL

You give everybody what he wants, including the opposition, and lo! there ain't no opposition.

DELL

It can be applied to all appropriation bills!

WINGBLATT

Yes, and I'm willing to bet it will be!

ALAN

I know I lost, Sol. You don't need to tell me.

DELL

Don't you feel bad about this, Mr. McClean.

SNEDEN

We made more mistakes than you did. We only won by accident!
[MISS MCMURTRY *enters.*

WINGBLATT

Why, you damn near beat us at our own game.
[*The crowd greets* MCMURTRY.

MCMURTRY

Mr. McClean, I want to thank you from my heart for the poor and the stricken who will turn to the bureau for relief!

SNEDEN

You aren't going to spurn us, are you, Bess?

MCMURTRY

Well, I don't as a rule—but on this occasion—
[*She takes a drink.* LEVERING *enters.*

LEVERING

Alan, my boy—many a man in Congress promises

more than he performs; but few indeed perform more than they promise. You're one of the few!

ALAN

You know I put those things in the bill to kill it!

WINGBLATT

But it didn't kill it. That's what put it through!

SNEDEN

And you were careful to stick in your own extra million, weren't you?

ALAN

I had a personal reason for doing that!

WINGBLATT

Well, so did we all! We all had personal reasons! Sol had his navy! Farnum had his national park! And I had—I won't say what I had, but it was damn good and personal!

LEVERING

We want you to come in and work with us, McClean.

ALAN

I'm afraid you're under a misapprehension. I'm not the kind of person to trust on the inside.

WINGBLATT

Oh, give us a whirl, brother. You can't buck the game single-handed. Are we going to celebrate?

FARNUM

Sit in with us a couple of months! You'll be the right kind of person!

LEVERING

You really have no choice now, McClean. You're one of us, or you have no friends in Congress.

ALAN

You want me in with you because I know too much and you're afraid I may tell what I know. Well, I'm not accepting the invitation.

PEEBLES

Does that mean you're thinking of letting newspaper correspondents in on confidential matters that took place in secret session?

ALAN

I don't know.

PEEBLES

That means he is.

WINGBLATT

Don't be a sorehead. We're quite willing to listen to suggestions. What do you think we ought to do?

ALAN

I think we all ought to get up and go home.

DELL

Go home!

ALAN

We've cost the country about four hundred millions today, and the least we can do is clear out of here before we cost them any more.

SNEDEN

You're suggesting that we all resign?

ALAN

I am.

FARNUM

Boys, am I losing my mind?

MCMURTRY

I never heard such talk!

WINGBLATT

Oh, I've had enough!

SNEDEN

I'm not much of a home boy myself!
[MARJORIE *and* GRAY *enter from the office.*

ALAN

How long do you think a governing body can go on
when it's made itself a laughing stock, the length and
breadth of the country, the way this one has?

WINGBLATT

Why, you simple-minded cub, that's treason!

ALAN

How can one speak treason about this government
or Congress? It's one vast, continuous, nation-wide
disaster!

EDDIE

Just another red, boys!

WINGBLATT

　A bull-fighter!

EDDIE

　He's following Ebner's trail!

ALAN

　And I'm not a red! I don't like communism or fascism or any other political patent medicine! If I did, I'd say what Ebner says—go right ahead the way you're going. You're doing all you can to bring it on!

FARNUM

　There's never been a better government on the face of the earth! Our forefathers fought and died to give us the government we have today!

ALAN

　And look at it now!

PEEBLES

　What he means is, he don't like us much.

GRAY

　You may not believe me, but I respect what you're trying to do—I respect it profoundly. Tell me what you would like to see here, Alan. If you know of anything better, I wouldn't mind working toward it myself. I don't care for this system any more than you do.

ALAN

　Is honesty possible here at all?

GRAY

　I'd say that honesty was so rare as to be almost unknown in any government, and impossible under our system.

PEEBLES

Now what the hell is our system?

GRAY

Our system is every man for himself—and the nation be damned!

SOL

And it works! It works when you give it a chance. Do you want me to point you the road to prosperity? Loot the treasury, loot the national resources, hang fortunes on the Wall Street Christmas tree! Graft, gigantic graft brought us our prosperity in the past and will lift us out of the present depths of parsimony and despair!

DELL

You're pushing it a little far, Sol!

SOL

I'm understating it! Brigands built up this nation from the beginning, brigands of a gigantic Silurian breed that don't grow in a piddling age like ours! They stole billions and gutted whole states and empires, but they dug our oil-wells, built our railroads, built up everything we've got, and invented prosperity as they went along! Let 'em go back to work! We can't have an honest government, so let 'em steal plenty and get us started again. Let the behemoths plunder so the rest of us can eat!

LEVERING

Oh, turn it off, Sol!

DELL

That don't sound so good!

GRAY

Allowing for Sol's usual exaggeration—it is true!

ALAN

Then aren't you against it?

GRAY

I am.

ALAN

And isn't it time to say that it can't go on?

FARNUM

Can't go on?

PEEBLES

Who's going to stop it?

WINGBLATT

Don Quixote!

SOL

Take it easy, boys. I heard Alan say once before that something couldn't go on, and the hell he raised gave you all heart-failure. If you've got anything on your mind, Alan, give us fair warning.

ALAN

More people are open-minded nowadays than you'd believe. A lot of them aren't so sure we found the

final answer a hundred and fifty years ago. Who
knows what's the best kind of government? Maybe
they all get rotten after a while and have to be replaced. It doesn't matter about you or me. We had
a little set-to here over a minor matter, and you've
won, but I want to tell you I'm not even a premoni-
tion of what you're going to hear crashing around
you if the voters who elect you ever find out what
you're like and what you do to them. The best I can
do is just to help them find it out.

EDDIE

Let him shoot his mouth off. He'll start talking wild
and the papers won't give him three lines.

SOL

That's true too, Alan. Nobody'll believe you. What
happens here is incredible, absolutely incredible.

ALAN

I'm not the person to give you a warning. I'm not a
politician. I'm a Nevada school-teacher. I don't know
your tricks—you showed me that tonight, and I won't
forget it. But I didn't lose because I was wrong. I
lost because I tried to beat you at your own game—
and you can always win at that. You think you're
good and secure in this charlatan's sanctuary you've
built for yourselves. You think the sacred and sense-
less legend poured into the people of this country
from childhood will protect you. It won't. It takes
about a hundred years to tire this country of trick-
ery—and we're fifty years overdue right now. That's
my warning. And I'd feel pretty damn pitiful and
lonely saying it to you, if I didn't believe there are

a hundred million people who are with me, a hundred million people who are disgusted enough to turn from you to something else. Anything else but this.
[*He turns and goes out.*

GRAY

And good luck to him!
[*He goes into his office.* MARJORIE *goes out after* ALAN.

LEVERING

Think the papers'll give him a break, Sol?

BUS

They'll give him a break! On every front page in the country!

SOL

They'll have to—if he hands them that line.

PEEBLES

May be a little nasty for some of us.

SOL

It'll blow over, it'll blow over. As a matter of fact, the natural resources of this country in political apathy and indifference have hardly been touched. They're just learning how to pay taxes. In a few more years you'll really give 'em taxes to pay.

WINGBLATT

You think so?

SOL

I know it. On the other hand, he's right about you.

I always told you boys you were a bunch of crooks, and you are. The whole blistering blasphemous batch of you! And some day they're going to catch up with you.

WINGBLATT

Well, how about yourself, you two-faced swindler?

SOL

I'm too old, Wingie. They won't get me. No—I don't hardly expect it in my time.
[*He pours himself a drink.*

BUS

Maybe.

CURTAIN